ARP 2343

/

NEW DIRECTIONS FOR HIGHER EDUCATION

Martin Kramer
EDITOR-IN-CHIEF

D1605886

Roles and Responsibilities of the Chief Financial Officer

Lucie Lapovsky
Mercy College

Mary P. McKeown-Moak
MGT of America, Inc.

EDITORS

Number 107, Fall 1999

JOSSEY-BASS PUBLISHERS
San Francisco

ROLES AND RESPONSIBILITIES OF THE CHIEF FINANCIAL OFFICER
Lucie Lapovsky, Mary P. McKeown-Moak (eds.)
New Directions for Higher Education, no. 107
Volume XXVII, Number 3
Martin Kramer, Editor-in-Chief

ISSN 0271-0560   ISBN 0-7879-4859-4

NEW DIRECTIONS FOR HIGHER EDUCATION is part of The Jossey-Bass Higher and Adult Education Series and is published quarterly by Jossey-Bass Inc., Publishers, 350 Sansome Street, San Francisco, California 94104–1342. Periodicals postage paid at San Francisco, California, and at additional mailing offices. Postmaster: Send address changes to New Directions for Student Services, Jossey-Bass Inc., Publishers, 350 Sansome Street, San Francisco, California 94104–1342.

SUBSCRIPTIONS cost $58.00 for individuals and $104.00 for institutions, agencies, and libraries. See Ordering Information page at end of book.

EDITORIAL CORRESPONDENCE should be sent to the Editor-in-Chief, Martin Kramer, 2807 Shasta Road, Berkeley, California 94104-1342.

Cover photograph and random dot by Richard Blair/Color & Light © 1990.

Jossey-Bass Web address: www.josseybass.com

Printed in the United States of America on acid-free recycled paper containing 100 percent recovered waste paper, of which at least 20 percent is postconsumer waste.

CONTENTS

EDITORS' NOTES

As the end of the twentieth century nears, higher education faces greater economic uncertainties than ever before. Demands for improved quality, increased competition for state and federal funds, the challenges of integrating technology into the curriculum, and changes in enrollment patterns have forced institutions of higher education to reexamine their missions. Colleges and universities have been challenged by some declines in resources and a reduction of public esteem. Financial well-being has never been assured for colleges and universities, and the future is not likely to be an exception.

The chief financial officer (CFO) of any institution of higher education stands squarely in the middle of the maelstrom. To the CFO fall the tasks of balancing the operating and capital budgets, planning for changes in the revenue mix, estimating enrollments, containing costs, investing the endowment wisely, and managing the institution's level of risk so that assets are protected. Clearly, CFOs need to keep many hats tucked away in the drawers of their desks to respond to the demands of changing customers, competitors, and technology.

This issue of *New Directions for Higher Education* addresses many of the issues faced each day by the CFO. For the new or experienced CFO, it provides insights and new methods for addressing issues. In the light of information about income, each college and university makes its own decisions about the scope and size of program offerings, program priorities, and institutional expenditure patterns. Each must also make decisions about the capital budget in addition to the current operating budget.

Enrollment management has become an issue critical to institutional survival. Although the declining enrollments projected for the final decade of the century did not occur, enrollments shifted. The proportion of traditional college-age students declined, and the number of part-time students increased. Student financial assistance appears to have played a critical role in enrollment management. Each college and university had to evaluate several issues. Would increased tuition charges decrease enrollments, and thus, reduce revenues? Would recruitment of certain types of students result in a reduction in net tuition revenues? Institutions became more aware of their ability to attract and retain students, and some sought assistance from professional marketing firms to sell their institution. In Chapter One, Lucie Lapovsky addresses the basic information that a CFO must know to understand how to work effectively with admissions and financial aid staff to maximize net tuition revenues and enroll an optimal class.

Especially critical in the role of the CFO is strategic budget planning. In Chapter Two, Kent John Chabotar addresses issues surrounding an effective budget process. Because the effectiveness of the budget process is dependent on the culture of the institution, Chabotar discusses a variety of budgets and explains the interrelationships among budgeting, planning, and financial modeling. What shall be the goal of the institution regarding faculty salaries? What is the expected faculty workload and student-faculty ratio? How much should be spent for staff benefits? For student financial assistance? Chabotar addresses these decisions in the context of the institutional culture.

At the same time that colleges and universities began to market themselves, pressures increased to contain costs. Institutions with strong endowments or increasing state appropriations were not immune to these economic exigencies. William S. Reed addresses cost containment issues in Chapter Three. How does a CFO help leadership not only to contain costs in the short run but also to reflect permanent changes in institutional operations and priorities? What would happen if the stock market went into a sustained decline? Or if students chose to opt for less expensive alternatives to a degree? Reed provides strategies for leadership in cost containment.

As any college or university faces cost containment issues, some components of the budget place enormous pressures on the CFO. Perhaps the biggest culprit (and one of the biggest consumers of any increases in a college's or university's revenues) is information technology. The technology environment is the most rapidly changing phenomenon that higher education has yet experienced. Computers now have useful lives of less than three years, end-user computing has significantly modified how campuses provide administrative data processing, and every faculty and staff member clamors for the most recent hardware and software. Will technology consume all available college resources? How does a college plan and budget rationally for information technology? In Chapter Four, Ellen F. Falduto provides strategies to plan and budget for the resource needs of technology. She provides helpful information on whether to lease or buy equipment and whether to outsource or use in-house services. Falduto contends that each CFO needs to develop a simple technology plan that is integrated with the institution's financial plan or budget.

In many colleges or universities, the costs of technology are financed in part by the endowment. In Chapter Five, William T. Spitz describes the critical policy decisions that must be made by the CFO to manage the endowment so that it can continue to be a major funding source for important campus initiatives. Spitz addresses issues of optimal manager structure and the role of the board investment committee in endowment management. He contends that the role of the CFO is to preserve the real value of the endowment through wise investment policy and to communicate effectively with the board investment committee.

Ronald E. Salluzzo might disagree with Janice M. Abraham's contention in Chapter Eight that risk management is most important, but he would not disagree that safeguarding the institution's assets is a critical role for the

CFO. In Chapter Six, he describes the use of the budget as an effective management tool. Is the institution financially healthy? Are sufficient revenues available to support the college's mission and plan? Salluzzo highlights development of a context for budget planning and a structure that permits communication of institutional direction to the entire college community.

Just as Salluzzo discusses the operational budget, J. Kent Caruthers and Daniel T. Layzell provide CFOs with useful practices for campus master planning and capital budgeting in Chapter Seven. How does the campus master plan relate to strategic planning, academic planning, and enrollment planning? How can a campus master plan contribute to institutional advancement? How can the capital budget be developed in a rational manner that integrates strategic planning? Caruthers and Layzell conclude that comprehensive institutional master planning can have profound impacts on the future success and viability of the institution. A well-conceived (and well-executed) campus master plan can assist in focusing scarce resources on quality programs that further achievement of the campus' mission.

Critical to endowment management is implementation of an appropriate risk management program. In Chapter Eight, Janice M. Abraham describes strategies to identify, manage, and transfer risk. In this context, risk encompasses not just financial risk in endowment management but also physical, casualty, liability, business, and reputational risk. Abraham provides help for the CFO in learning not only how to control risk but also how to reduce risk and understand liability issues. The multifaceted role of the CFO is to identify risk, develop plans to reduce and control risk, transfer risk to others, and track and report the costs of risk management. Abraham asserts that the most important role the CFO plays is risk management to safeguard the assets of the institution.

As higher education becomes more competitive and as controlling costs becomes critical in focusing scarce resources on quality programs, many colleges and universities have begun to use consortial relationships. Consortia can provide program enrichment, cost avoidance, and cost reductions. In Chapter Nine, Mary Jo Maydew describes the benefits and also the pitfalls of consortia. She provides as a case study the example of Five Colleges, Inc., one of the oldest and most successful consortia and identifies the advantages and challenges of consortial relationships.

In Chapter Ten, Mary P. McKeown-Moak describes the advantages, disadvantages, and types of funding formulas used by states in the budgetary process. Do funding formulas ensure an equitable allocation of resources among institutions? Can formulas ensure provision of adequate resources? Do formulas foster institutional accountability? McKeown-Moak provides answers to these questions and includes methods for positioning the campus to minimize the disadvantages of formula budgeting.

Another hat worn by the CFO is that of lobbyist or governmental relations specialist. In Chapter Eleven, William F. Lasher, Gwen Grigsby, and Charlotte Sullivan highlight the role of the CFO in working with the state legislature, pitfalls in legislative relations, and special problems faced by institutions located in capital cities. At a time when the general public and legislators are demanding more accountability for public funds, colleges and universities must build positive relationships with state government. CFOs have a critical role in providing data and in providing an institutional context to inform public policy and decision making.

Finally, in Chapter Twelve, Thomas Anderes describes the practical applications of using peer institutions as one component in financial and budgetary decision making processes. What criteria should be used to select a set of peers? Should the peers include aspirational peers, that is, institutions that represent what the CFO's institution would like to become? What roles will peer institutions play in establishing budgets, determining salaries and setting workloads and other variables for your institution? The use of peer institutional data to establish points of reference seems to be an inevitable outcome of the pressure for increased accountability.

Lucie Lapovsky
Mary P. McKeown-Moak
Editors

LUCIE LAPOVSKY is president of Mercy College in New York and chair of the NACUBO institutional student aid advisory committee. She was vice president for finance at Goucher College, Maryland.

MARY P. MCKEOWN-MOAK is senior associate at MGT of America, Inc., Austin, Texas. She was until recently senior financial officer of the Arizona University System.

1

Enrollment management is critical to the success of all colleges. This chapter provides the basic information that a CFO must know to effectively understand how to work with the admissions and financial aid professionals at the college to maximize net tuition revenue and enroll the optimal class.

What You Need to Know
About Enrollment Management

Lucie Lapovsky

Have you and your board agonized over the tuition increase and finally agreed to raise it 5 percent? Has the admissions director proudly announced that the freshman class was not only larger than the budgeted number by 10 percent but also smarter than had been projected? Were the board and the president excited about the positive outlook for the next year? Was the faculty suddenly expecting that there would be additional revenue to start new projects? This is often the case when the chief financial officer (CFO) finds that the net tuition revenue available for the year is actually less than was budgeted. This is not a pretty situation for the CFO or the institution.

How does this anomalous result occur? Quite simply, more has been spent on financial aid to enroll the class than has been budgeted. This situation occurs often but can be avoided. This chapter uses data from the National Association of College and University Business Officers (NACUBO) Institutional Financial Aid Survey to provide information on various changes in enrollments and net tuition revenues experienced by institutions. The chapter also offers guidance on how the CFO can effectively participate in the enrollment management process and how modeling techniques can be used to help ensure desired outcomes.

Traditionally, the CFO and the board concentrate on establishing tuition levels. Significant time is spent recommending the appropriate tuition increase and calculating how it will provide additional revenue for the following year. Institutions usually consider tuition levels at their peer institutions, those institutions that resemble them closely, as well as at competitor institutions, that is, those institutions that compete against them for the same students. Each year the president and the public relations office labor over the annual letter to parents discussing the tuition increase for next year and explaining why it is necessary and what it will allow the institution to accomplish.

In reality, often little relationship exists between the change in tuition rates and *net tuition*, which is defined here as the published tuition price minus the average institutional financial aid per student. Figure 1.1 uses NACUBO data to show the relationship between published tuition and net tuition in fall 1998 for freshmen. Each point in Figure 1.1 represents several institutions; over three hundred independent four-year institutions are included in these data.

There is a wide range in the relationship between tuition and net tuition. For example, among institutions with a published tuition of $10,000, the net tuition ranges from less than $5,000 to just under $10,000. The differences in the relationship between net tuition and published tuition reflect the college's institutional financial aid or discounting policies. The tuition and net tuition are equal in only two institutions in this sample; these are represented by points on the diagonal line in Figure 1.1. These institutions do not offer any institutional financial aid; their tuition discount rate, the institutional aid per student divided by the tuition, is 0 percent. There are fifty-five institutions, 15 percent of the total, where net tuition is less than 50 percent of the published tuition rate.

Boards always agonize over the increase in tuition and worry over how the public will perceive the increase. Figure 1.2 displays the relationship between the change from fall 1997 to fall 1998 in tuition and net tuition for freshmen; it is provided to further illustrate that concentrating on the change in tuition is not the appropriate focus for understanding the financial implications of a change in tuition on the institution or on the students.

Figure 1.1. Published Tuition versus Net Tuition, Fall 1998

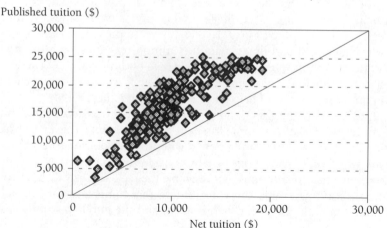

Published tuition ($)

Of the 367 institutions in this database, 348 increased tuition between 1997 and 1998, 80 of which experienced decreases in net tuition per student. This result occurs when the amount of institutional financial aid awarded per student increases more than the increase in tuition. Of those 80 institutions, 33 had increases in net freshman revenue. This situation occurs when enrollment increases to offset the decrease in net tuition per student.

Only six independent institutions in this database reduced tuition between 1997 and 1998; net tuition per student declined at five of them. The institution that experienced an increase in net tuition reduced tuition 28 percent, and yet net tuition per freshman increased 17 percent because the college reduced its financial aid per student more than the reduction in tuition. Thirteen institutions held tuition at the 1997 level; seven experienced increases in net tuition, and six had decreases in net tuition per student. At these thirteen institutions, net tuition per student actually increased an average of 3.8 percent.

These data are meant to reinforce the point that the CFO and the board need to be as concerned with institutional aid policies as they are with establishing the tuition rate. An increase in tuition may result in a reduction in net tuition per student, depending on the institution's financial aid policies.

To make the matter even more complex, the impact on net tuition revenues will be influenced by the change in enrollment at the institution.

Figure 1.2. Percent Change in Tuition and Net Tuition: 1997–98

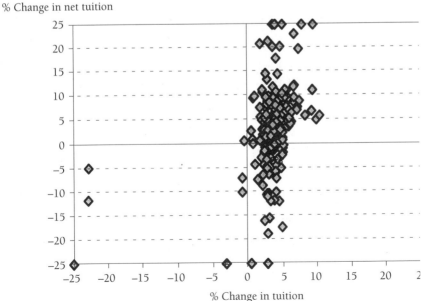

Between 1997 and 1998, freshman enrollment increased 2.4 percent over-all at the 367 independent institutions in the NACUBO database while tuition increased 4.1 percent and net tuition increased 3.3 percent (Table 1.1).

Among these institutions, freshman enrollment increased at 222 institutions (60 percent), tuition increased at 348 institutions (95 percent) and net tuition increased at 275 institutions (75 percent). In addition, net freshman revenue increased at 253 institutions (69 percent). Figures 1.3 and 1.4 display the relationships between change in net tuition and change in full-time freshman enrollment and between freshman enrollment and net freshman revenue, respectively. Among the 222 institutions that had increases in the number of freshmen between 1997 and 1998, tuition increased at 211 (95 percent).

At the 211 institutions with enrollment and tuition increases, net tuition increased at 155 (73 percent). All of the institutions with increases in freshman enrollment, tuition, and net tuition had increases in net revenue from freshmen. Of the 64 institutions (17 percent) with increases in freshman enrollment and decreases in net tuition between 1997 and 1998, 39 (61 percent) had increases in net freshman revenue.

Among the 145 institutions that experienced no change in freshman enrollment or enrollment decreases between 1997 and 1998, 3 reduced tuition, 3 kept tuition at the 1997 rate, and the remaining 139 institutions increased tuition. Of the 6 institutions that did not increase tuition, 2 experienced a decrease in net tuition and 4 had decreases in net freshman revenue. Of the 139 institutions with freshman enrollment declines and tuition increases, 25 (18 percent) experienced decreases in net tuition and 84 (60 percent) experienced decreases in net freshmen revenue. Forty percent of the institutions with enrollment decreases and tuition increases experienced increases in net freshman revenue. Clearly, these institutions had a very high likelihood of improved finances for the freshman class as they had no enrollment-related workload increases.

Between 1997 and 1998, 253 (69 percent) of the institutions experienced increases in net freshman revenue. Of these 253 institutions, 200 had increases in freshman enrollment, and 215 had increases in net freshman tuition. Of the 114 institutions with decreases in net freshman revenue

**Table 1.1. Summary Enrollment and Tuition Data
NACUBO 1998 Institutional Financial Aid Survey**

	1997	1998	% Change
Average freshman enrollment	482	493	2.4
Average tuition	$14,220	$14,829	4.1
Average net tuition	$8,946	$9,247	3.3

between 1997 and 1998, 24 had increases in freshman enrollment, and 60 had increases in net freshman tuition.

What Is the Relationship of Enrollment Management to Institutional Quality?

An institution's quality is dependent on the quality of both its student body and its programs. An institution explicitly determines how much to spend on each of these. A few of the most selective institutions in the country are able to get the quality of the student body they want without any expenditures for financial aid. These institutions choose to provide financial aid to some students to diversify the economic characteristics of their student body. Most other institutions must provide aid not only to students who are unable to afford the institution but also to students who are unwilling to attend the institution at the published price. These tend to be the institution's better students, and the institution usually chooses to provide aid to them to elevate the quality of the student body. Thus, most institutions today are providing both need-based and characteristic- or merit-based student aid.

The more an institution spends on aiding its student body, the less the institution will have available to fund programs. Explicit trade-offs must be

Figure 1.3. Percent Change in Net Tuition and Percent Change in the Number of Full-Time Freshmen

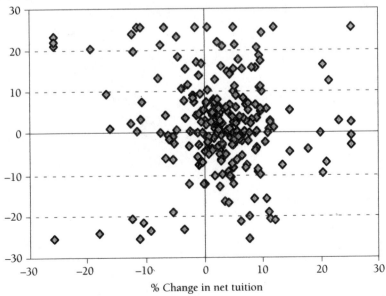

% Change in net tuition

made between the required net tuition revenue, the size and type of the student body, and the amount of funding that will be available for programs.

What Should the CFO Do?

All of the preceding data have been presented to make it very clear that if CFOs want a stake in determining net tuition revenues and resource allocations, they must become involved in enrollment management. I say enrollment management rather than institutional financial aid policies because I believe that it is critical for CFOs to be involved in the entire mix of policies involved. The preceding data are also intended to illustrate that controlling financial aid will not necessarily result in the desired net tuition revenue because financial aid impacts enrollment.

The Enrollment Management Task Force

An enrollment management task force is recommended to effectively oversee and coordinate enrollment and financial aid. The task force should include, at a minimum, the CFO, the chief enrollment management officer (if there is one), the director of admissions, the director of financial aid, and the director of institutional research. Beyond this group, depending on insti-

Figure 1.4. Percent Change in Full-time Freshmen and Percent Change in Net Freshmen Revenue: 1997–98

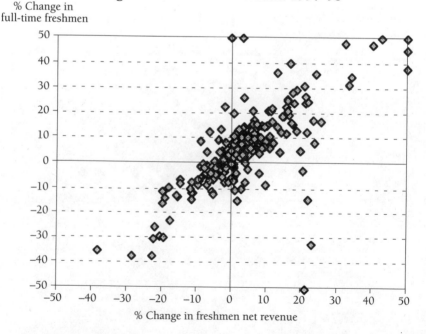

% Change in full-time freshmen

% Change in freshmen net revenue

tutional culture, a few faculty representatives also may be included. This task force will make the strategic decisions that deal with the size and composition of the class, as well as the trade-offs involved in recruiting it. The task force will also establish the strategic uses of financial aid to minimize the net cost of attracting the class.

The task force should begin by assessing the admissions funnel, which begins with the inquiry pool, the number of students who express an interest in finding out about the college. The task force should then progress to the applicant pool, those students who actually apply to the institution. A college wants to have a high *conversion rate*—that is, a high number of those inquiring who actually apply.

Table 1.2 displays information for a hypothetical institution and data on its peer institutions. It is advisable to benchmark throughout the process to assess efficiency compared with similar institutions. In this example, the institution has 28,500 inquiries and 2,000 applicants. This provides a conversion rate of 7 percent whereas the peers have a conversion rate of 9 percent. A higher conversion rate is better because an institution spends money dealing with each inquiry.

In this example, the hypothetical institution accepts 1,650 students, or 83 percent of its applicant pool, while the peers accept 75 percent of their applicant pools. A decision on the number of students to accept is guided by the number of qualified applicants as well as the projected yield rate to get down to the desired number of students who ultimately enroll at the institution. In this example, the yield at the hypothetical institution is 28 percent; at the peer institutions 30 percent. Finally, the discount rate for the class should be examined. At the hypothetical institution, the discount rate is 41 percent compared with 38 percent at the peers.

Clearly, this example demonstrates several points. First, the hypothetical institution has a more difficult time enrolling its class and spends more

Table 1.2. Assessment of Applicant Pool and Enrollment Results

	Hypothetical Institution	Peers (%)
Inquiries	28,5000	
Applicants	2,000	
Conversion	7%	9
Accepted	1,650	
Acceptance rate	83%	75
Enrolled	465	
Yield	28%	30
Discount rate	41%	38

to get its class than its peer institutions. This implies that the peer institutions, all other things being equal, will have more funds available for programmatic initiatives.

Table 1.2 does not demonstrate anything about how the discount rate was used to get this class; Table 1.3 provides information to assess how the hypothetical institution spent its financial aid funds.

Most institutions rank their applicant pool and give each applicant a reader rating. The applicant pool of the hypothetical institution is divided into four ratings, A through D, with A being those students that the institution most wants to enroll (although every school will define an A student differently) and D being those students who are least desirable.

In this example, the 2,000 applicants are divided into groups by reader rating as shown in Table 1.3. The hypothetical college admits all of the A's and B's, most of the C's, and 40 percent of the D's. The yield of the admitted students and the discount rate for each reader rating are quite different. The yield and discount rate for A students is the highest. The college had to discount the A students' tuition by 75 percent to get them to enroll. By comparison, the yield on the C students is 24 percent, and they have a discount rate of only 15 percent. The yield on the D students is 40 percent, and their discount rate is 30 percent.

The questions to ask are: Were financial aid dollars spent wisely to get the desired class? Could financial aid have been redistributed to change the size and composition of the class? What would have happened with a lower discount rate? What would have been the net tuition revenue for the class and the characteristics of the class?

Table 1.4 shows how the hypothetical college distributed financial aid to individual students who enrolled. For example, no A student who enrolled at this institution paid the published price of $12,000. An A student required a discount rate of at least 50 percent to enroll, and some were given a 100 percent discount. This is the type of analysis the CFO should do each year to see what it takes to enroll a class and what changes might be needed. Table 1.4 also shows that the net tuition paid by students is

Table 1.3. Assessment of Applicant Pool by Reader Rating

	Reader Rating				
	A	B	C	D	Total
Applicants	300	600	600	500	2,000
Admits	300	600	550	200	1,650
Acceptance rate	100%	100%	92%	40%	83%
Enrolled	135	120	130	80	465
Yield	45%	20%	24%	40%	28%
Discount rate	75%	38%	15%	30%	41%

$7,080, but the amount varied considerably by rating of student. The average tuition paid by A students is $3,000 compared with $7,440 for B students, $10,200 for C students, and $8,400 for D students.

Questions that the CFO might want to explore include the following: Did the college need to award full tuition scholarships to any students, or would they have enrolled with less aid? What if the college had discounted somewhat more to C students and somewhat less to D students? Would the college have increased the quality of the class at the same expenditure? Could or should the college have accepted more D students while reducing the aid to them and still have enrolled the number of students projected, with less financial aid? These are just a few of the questions that the CFO should be asking.

As can be seen from this example, enrollment management today is a very complex strategic process. Each institution wants to maximize enrollment of the students it deems most desirable at the least cost in terms of institutional financial aid. In economic terms, an institution wants to milk the demand curve. To accomplish this, fairly sophisticated modeling of the yields for different types of applicants is required. Among students who are interested in attending an institution, some are willing and able to pay the published tuition price, some are willing but unable to pay the tuition, and some are able but unwilling to pay the tuition.

Colleges need to be able to distinguish among these groups of students and then decide how much the college wants each individual student by determining how much institutional aid it would be willing to provide that student to improve the probability that he or she will enroll. Implementing this to the fullest can often conflict with an institution's values. For example, an institution may be more attractive to students who live within fifty miles of the campus. Therefore, to equalize the probability of enrollment for

Table 1.4. Analysis of Freshman Class Reader Rating by Net Tuition

Net Tuition ($)	Quality Rating				Total	
	A	B	C	D	No.	%
12,000 (Full pay)	—	—	20	22	42	9.0
10,000–11,999	—	—	71	19	90	19.4
8,000–9,999	—	42	24	9	75	16.1
6,000–7,999	—	68	10	7	85	18.3
4,000–5,999	23	5	3	8	39	8.4
2,000–3,999	90	4	1	7	102	21.9
1–1,999	20	1	1	8	30	6.5
0	2	—	—	—	2	0.4
Total	135	120	130	80	465	100.0
Average net tuition ($)	3,000	7,440	10,200	8,400	7,080	

two students who share all of the same characteristics except place of residence, the college would provide more institutional aid to the student who lives farther from the campus. This may not be acceptable to the institution.

Some institutions find that they need to award more aid to men than women with similar characteristics to equalize the yield of the two groups. Institutions often will stop short of the true revenue maximization solution because they are unwilling to treat similar students differently.

Which Is Better: A Discount or a Lower Price?

The NACUBO database indicates that more than 33 percent of the independent institutions provide institutional financial aid to more than 90 percent of their students. Does this indicate that these institutions should just lower their tuition? It may, but a lower price is not necessarily the best policy to maximize net revenue.

For example, although an institution may give almost all its students some aid, the amount of the aid given to individual students is likely to differ significantly. The higher published price provides an institution with greater ability to provide different amounts of aid, depending on the student's characteristics.

Another argument advanced against price reduction is that some people still believe in what is known as the "Chivas Regal effect," which is based on the assumption that people believe the higher the price of the good or the service, the higher the quality. If this is true, a reduction in the price of the college can result in a decline in the demand for the college.

Might a high price keep some people from applying to the institution? Maybe. One strategy that several institutions are using to reduce the number of prospective students who are scared off by a high published price is to publicly announce that a student with certain characteristics will receive a scholarship from the institution. For example, some institutions will give full tuition scholarships to any students who rank number one or two in their high school class. Others are trying to provide earlier information to those who are unable to pay the published price as to what it will cost. For example, Princeton placed a financial aid estimator on its web site to provide estimates of what a family will have to contribute to a student's education there.

Discounting Policies and Institutional Capacity

All analysis of discounting should take into account the relationship of the current enrollment to institutional capacity. If an institution is below capacity, the marginal cost of additional students is far less than when an institution is at or above capacity. An institution risks far less if it overawards aid and has an unexpected increase in enrollment when it has room to spare. When the institution is at capacity, this same result can be disastrous because not only can net revenue per student decline but institutional costs can also increase.

When the institution is below capacity, it has far more ability to experiment with aid policies and yields. When an institution is at capacity and is trying to increase net revenues, it needs to trade off a more highly subsidized student for one who requires a lower subsidy to enroll.

Conclusions

The point of this chapter is to impress CFOs with the importance of direct involvement in enrollment management policies. It is critical that boards and their finance committees understand the need to look beyond tuition to net tuition revenues in order to truly improve the financial health of the institution. Is there a correct relationship between tuition and net tuition revenue? No. As the data indicate, institutions operate with great variations in the relationship between these two variables. What is critical is that an institution needs sufficient tuition revenue to be able to provide quality programs. More revenue is always better than less revenue.

References

Breneman, D., Lapovsky, L., and Myers, D. "Private College Pricing: Are Current Policies Sustainable?" *The Forum for the Future of Higher Education,* 1999.

Lapovsky, L. "Tuition Discounting Continues to Climb." NACUBO *Business Officer,* 1996, 29(8), 20.

Lapovsky, L. "Phantom Dollars." NACUBO *Business Officer,* 1997, 30(9), 23.

Lapovsky, L. "Wisdom Needed." NACUBO *Business Officer,* 1998, 31(8), 17.

Lapovsky, L. "An Enrollment Management Tool." NACUBO *Business Officer,* 1999, 32(9), 25–31.

LUCIE LAPOVSKY *is president of Mercy College in New York and chair of the NACUBO institutional student aid advisory committee. She was vice president for finance at Goucher College, Maryland.*

2

An effective budget process is dependent on the culture of the institution. Different processes and different types of budgets are appropriate depending on the institution. This chapter discusses a variety of budgets and explains the interrelationships between budgeting, planning, and financial modeling.

How to Develop an Effective Budget Process

Kent John Chabotar

Colleges and universities usually view a budget as a one-year spending plan that identifies the sources and uses of funds. But a budget can also serve a strategic function as a fundamental statement of priorities and beliefs. It tells a story about not only how much money is earned and spent but also which goals and activities are truly most important to the institution.

- A president or chancellor may speak about a new town-gown initiative, or a dean may announce a reform of financial aid policy. Both proposals are no more than that, proposals, until the budget provides the funds to implement them.
- Claims that instruction is a top priority are less convincing when the budget allocation for instruction, in dollars or in percentage of total, has been declining.
- A need-blind admissions policy may be inspiring but meaningless without sufficient endowment or other revenues.

If legislators, parents, and students want to learn what a college or university really values, they should remember the advice of the character in the movie *Jerry Maguire:* "Show me the money."

Technical Aspects

This year's budget is the key factor in preparing next year's budget. Budgeting tends to be incremental, a process of adding to and subtracting from an existing budget, rather than the comprehensive, zero-based approach that scholars advocate and chief financial officers (CFOs) often desire. A multi-year budget or financial plan may be especially useful. If the current budget contains preliminary estimates of next year's budget, use them as a starting point.

Sources of Information. Check with other administrators, consult with faculty and staff associations, legislators, and trustees, and collect as much information and advice as possible on resources, priorities, new programs, and other budget drivers. Enrollment ceilings, position controls, salary savings targets, and midyear reductions may limit budget discretion.

In public institutions, the budget process must also conform to state requirements. Budgets may be formula driven by the numbers of faculty and students or square footage. Cooperation with the state is essential to secure adequate government appropriations or to issue bonds.

Finally, the essence of strategic budgeting is its explicit link to the institution's strategic plan.

- The board can state this vision in a formal plan with a mission statement, goals, objectives, and programs. Budgeting is done at the program level and rolled up to estimate costs of the objectives, goals, and mission.
- A plan also can be organic, developing and changing over time and supplemented by periodic statements of intermediate-term academic or administrative priorities.

Such clear ends for the institution—whether formal or informal—are essential ingredients for programming and budgeting most effectively. In a sense, the budget becomes the plan with dollar signs added.

Types of Budgets. College budgets are based on objects of expenditure—salaries, benefits, utilities, and other goods and services—that the institution purchases. Higher education officials view such detail as concrete, understandable, and useful for controlling spending. Some budgets even list authorized numbers of desks or typewriters that employees may buy during the fiscal year. College- or universitywide budget ceilings are delineated finally by administrative or academic department. An *object budget* answers the question, What are we buying?

A *program budget* starts with object-level detail but organizes data not only by department but also by program. Instruction, research, academic support, student services, operations and maintenance of the physical plant, and institutional support (administrative overhead) are the most significant programs. The program budget answers the question, What are we trying to do?

Responsibility center budgets attribute revenues and expenditures to each school and department and allocate to each a share of general institutional overhead. This type of budget attempts to decentralize management and accountability and to make colleges and schools more responsible for their own budgets. Many fear that responsibility center budgeting favors profitability over mission and program. Yet it does allow CFOs and others to compare costs and performance across the institution. That a mission-critical department requires a subsidy is not a problem; not knowing that a subsidy is needed is a problem. Questions here are Who is doing the spending? and Which units require subsidies to survive?

Presentation. The best budget presentations separate the base budget from *incremental* additions and deletions. The *base budget* is the current budget plus or minus contractual or legal obligations (for example, debt service, or collective bargaining agreements). Incremental additions to the budget might include discretionary increases in salaries or benefits, authorized positions, and operating expenses. Deletions of staff or operating expenses—often needed during retrenchment or simply to balance the budget—are presented separately. Sometimes the total budget can be the same or even increased by boosting some department budgets while cutting others, an art called "growth by substitution."

Budgets separate operating from capital needs, too. The *operating budget* funds day-to-day activities over one or two years. The *capital budget* oversees buildings and grounds over the longer, four- to five-year period needed to plan and execute construction or major maintenance projects.

Budgets also present the sources of revenue. The usual convention is to show the largest revenues first (for example, student fees in a liberal arts college and government appropriations for a state university). Sometimes the budget does not show student aid as an expenditure but as a discount against tuition (as a contrarevenue). Trustees like this approach because in the businesses with which most of them are familiar, gross sales are not as important as net revenue after discounts and materials costs are deducted. Net tuition revenue has the same cachet in higher education.

Financial Planning Models. Financial planning models forecast revenues and expenses; they take five to ten years to detect the future implications of the current budget. Planning models reveal how even small percentage increases to student fees or employee salaries compound quickly over time. Forecasting assumptions must be clear and convincing, and they must include items such as inflation, annual fund and capital campaign expectations, levels of state appropriations, and formula funding. The plan can confirm or discourage the institution's ambitions before scarce resources are committed. Figure 2.1 shows how each source of revenue can be projected as part of a financial planning model. Check on the reliability of the model by going back three to five years and pretending that you do not know the actual revenues and expenses today. Which forecasting assumption would have most accurately predicted net tuition revenue, appropriations, annual giving, and other budget items? Use the results of this analysis to fine-tune the model going forward.

Budgeting Process

How a budget is decided also is important. Many CFOs feel comfortable with a top-down approach in which the administration and board prepare

Figure 2.1. Financial Planning Projection

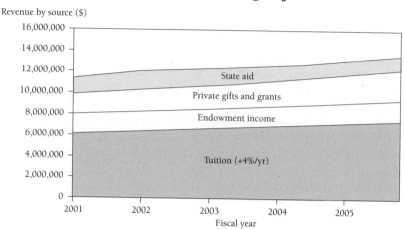

Revenue by source ($)

the budget. This is particularly true for public institutions that share power with state agencies. The budget is viewed as too technical and complicated for faculty and staff and students to understand. The budget process is a black box, and budget decisions are announced after the fact.

Approaches. Yet a campus community is more likely to understand and accept a budget that it helped to develop. A budgeting process can be made educational by introducing everyone to the terms and concepts of financial management. The rationale for priorities may become clearer. The budget also may be better informed and more accurately reflect campus realities. Three other approaches engage the community in the budgeting process to an increasingly greater extent:

- An *informational* approach provides periodic updates to faculty and staff about the process and decisions. The administration announces data about probable revenues and budget priorities through memoranda and regular meetings but does not solicit feedback.
- Others are experimenting with a *consultative approach* in which opinions about the budget are actively sought and debated. The president may ask for input at a faculty meeting or student government conference or from individuals. Their ideas sometimes alter decisions about tuition increases, endowment spending rates, and other budget drivers.
- In the most *participative approach,* faculty and staff draft the budget, typically by forming a committee and holding hearings, and recommend the budget to the president and trustees.

In a participative process, the committee's authority should be defined at the start to avoid unrealistic expectations. The committee should be charged with recommending the budget to the president or other campus chief executive. The president then may decide to recommend the budget to the board or legislature or to amend or reject it without consulting the committee again. Additionally, the president may impose goals or constraints. For example, the committee may be expected to develop a budget that is balanced, invests an increasing proportion of the total budget on the academic program, limits tuition increases to consumer price inflation, and if cutbacks become necessary, maintains the existing number of faculty positions.

When the participative approach works, it works well indeed. In 1991, Bowdoin College established a budget and financial priorities committee amidst a severe budget crisis marked by $1–$4 million annual deficits. The committee represents the student body, faculty, administrative and support staff, and senior officers. They recommend not only long-term priorities about all aspects of campus life, including academic programs, facilities maintenance, and information technology, but also how to fund them. A faculty member is committee chair, and the college treasurer is vice chair. The committee's effectiveness was proven in February 1999 when the board of trustees enacted the college's seventh consecutive balanced budget.

As the approach evolves from the informational to participative, however, the process becomes slower. It takes time to prepare user-friendly communications materials for the campus, organize meetings and other vehicles for obtaining reactions, and answer many questions and suggestions. The time factor may be a big impediment to participative budgeting in public institutions that already have a twelve- to sixteen-month budget cycle due to the involvement of state agencies.

Cultural Fit. If the institutional culture tends to be inclusive about most issues—with faculty and staff sitting on committees with real decision-making power—an inclusive budgeting process will not be that startling. On the other hand, where power has been centralized in the administration, occasional budgetary consultation should precede widespread participation, and any change should be well explained and gradual.

A gradual method is to start participative budgeting at the department or division level. For example, a dining services director might involve supervisors and staff throughout the department in preparing their recommended budget although the college process as a whole is much less participative. Differences in decision-making styles should not preclude involvement in the budget process in a department that wants it.

Community Involvement. Community meetings characterize both consultative and participative approaches. These meetings may be all-campus at a small college or all-school at a large university. What should be discussed?

- Budget process and context (for example, legislative mandates, building programs, economic conditions, and new programs)

- Major budget choices (for example, tuition and fees, endowment earnings, state appropriations, salaries and wages, operations and maintenance of the physical plant, and financial aid)
- Feedback about the draft budget in time to make changes before its submission to the chief executive and governing board and
- Results of executive and board action (to answer the question, who got what?).

All meetings should encourage two-way communication. Participants should not only hear progress reports but also have an opportunity to speak. The committee might solicit reactions to a list, distributed in advance, of revenue and expense options under consideration. Be aware of how public meeting laws affect the timing and content of these meetings.

Another option is to use e-mail and the campus Intranet to convey this information. Consider posting the budget on the institution's web site and soliciting opinions via cyberspace. A chat room might be established in which the CFO might discuss key budget issues.

Never underestimate the unfamiliarity of the campus with financial terms and concepts, which can contribute to rampant suspicion that the accountants are hiding the money. One response might have the finance vice president or a knowledgeable faculty member offer workshops on budget practices, financial statements, and the precepts of cost containment. Just be sure that budget materials are written clearly and define critical terms. For example, a miniglossary might be a standard part of your financial report, as shown in Exhibit 2.1.

Role of the Board. A core responsibility of the institution's governing board (trustees, regents, and legislative committees) is approval of the annual budget. Among the questions boards should ask about the budget are:

- How does the recommended budget articulate with the mission and long-term financial plan?
- What long-term capital and other commitments does the budget entail, and do sufficient revenues exist to cover them?
- What contingencies exist in the budget, and how does the institution propose to handle unexpected shifts in revenues or expenses during the year?

Most boards have finance committees that review and hopefully recommend the budget to the full board. The CFO should consult this committee two or three times during the process about the major budget components and campus concerns. The committee chair should be consulted more frequently. The finance committee's chief role should be to contemplate how various budget options affect not only next year's budget but also the institution's long-term financial outlook. For example, what will be the impact in ten years of an annual spending rate of 5 percent of the endowment's market value?

Exhibit 2.1. A Financial Report Miniglossary

Colleges and other nonprofits have a peculiar "budgetspeak" that should be translated into English before the new reader continues. The *operating budget* earns most of its revenues from student fees and endowment earnings (and in the case of public colleges, state appropriations). The *endowment* grows by prudent investments and new gifts; it is depleted primarily by spending in support of the operating budget that the board's spending policy limits to a targeted average of market value.

The budget's major *expenditures* can be classified by function (e.g., instruction, student services) and by object (e.g., salaries, fringe benefits). Because they are directly related to the college's mission, many budget functions such as instruction are grouped as *educational and general* (E&G). Other support functions, such as dining services, summer programs, and the bookstore, are grouped separately on the budget as *auxiliary enterprises*. *Depreciation* (allowance for wear and tear on buildings and other capital assets) is not included as a budget expenditure, but it is recognized on the college's annual financial statements, if the college is private.

Both revenues and expenditures are classified either as *restricted* (limited by the donor to specified purposes such as financial aid or faculty positions) or *unrestricted*. The term *designated* usually means that the board sets aside unrestricted funds for specific purposes (e.g., debt service and operating costs on a building).

In addition, the process should engage board committees with substantive oversight in areas such as academic affairs, student life, and facilities. They may resent allowing the finance committee to monopolize budget decisions that may profoundly affect their areas of responsibility. The CFO should update each substantive committee about the budget outlook for its area. For example, the academic affairs committee might review faculty numbers and salary pools. The CFO should also update the committees about the context of the institution's total budget and other priorities to minimize "special pleading."

Besides informing the budget process, involving board committees supplies the administration with multiple opportunities to convince committee members before they debate and vote on the budget at the meeting of the full board.

Strategic Indicators

A budget can be seen as a statement of input, a summary of resources invested into the organization. The concerns focus on control: whether the budget was balanced at the end of the fiscal year, whether individual schools and departments hit their budget targets, and whether the budget met the intent of legislators and donors. A *strategic* budget also focuses on whether the money spent achieved anything of value. These achievements can be end-result outcomes or, more likely, key indicators that show the budget's relevance to intermediate financial and program goals.

Efficiency and Productivity. Budgets are frequently correlated with staffing and workload statistics. For example, the CFO may study the relationship between an academic department's budget and its enrollment, average class size, student-faculty ratio, and teaching load.

Student and Educational Outcomes. Students and parents appear willing to pay for a college education, some claim, because it is an excellent investment. A person with a college degree can expect to earn far more than the typical high school graduate. To this end, institutions monitor student retention, graduation, and employment rates.

Ideally, though, colleges and universities should correlate budgets with gains in instruction, research, and service. Measurement seems easier for scholarly activity (for example, the number of grants applications funded or the number of scholarly works published) than for education. Does the university, for example, achieve the promised results on student cohorts A, B, and C by expending $X on Y program? Most institutions are unable to justify their costs with the measurable outcomes of a course or degree program. This mystifies corporate leaders who serve on governing boards and are accustomed to stringent market and profitability tests for their products and services.

Financial Outcomes. More realistically, the institution can detect whether the budget supports its vision and priorities without necessarily evaluating results.

- Affordability is evinced by the share of total revenue supplied by student fees and how financial aid policies have affected net revenue.
- Trends in revenue earned from government appropriations and annual giving suggest external support.
- Government- and foundation-sponsored programs imply the centrality of research.
- The proportion of the budget spent on instruction and on academic support such as libraries and information technology suggests the importance of teaching.
- Expenses for student services and auxiliary enterprises such as dining and dormitories suggest the quality of student life.
- Expenses incurred for operation and maintenance of the physical plant as well as new construction and other capital projects demonstrate the preservation of physical assets.
- Preservation of human assets can be indicated by expenses for employee training, tuition reimbursement, and compensation for faculty and staff, including fringe benefits.

Analyzing financial outcomes in nominal as well as constant (inflation-adjusted) dollars can be both interesting and informative. Apparently huge increases in any of the above indicators may become decreases when inflation is added to the equation. Figure 2.2 depicts how costs per student

Figure 2.2. E&G Cost per Student (FY 1988–89 to FY 1998–99)

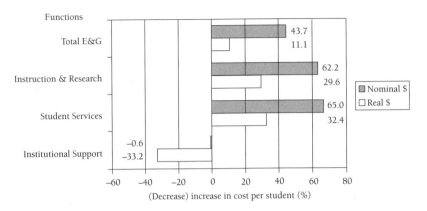

seemed to skyrocket over ten years when expressed in nominal dollars; for example, instruction and research increased by 62 percent. Adjusting for inflation slashes these increases by half and actually slashes the real per student costs for institutional support by a third.

Financial Distress. How can a college or university detect a financial crisis? The prevailing measure to look for is a deficit in the annual operating budget. Sporadic small deficits are often no cause for alarm, and neither is a large deficit in one year if sufficient reserves or endowment exist to cover it. Institutions should take action when the deficits increase in consecutive years or become greater than 5 to 10 percent of operating revenues.

Colleges and universities may have severe cash flow problems despite a balanced budget. Meeting payroll and other short-term expenses can be a challenge when cash inflows surge two or three times each year when students and parents pay tuition bills. During economic downturns, state governments may encounter slower or lower tax collections that pressure the cash flows of public institutions and sometimes result in midyear revertments of revenues.

As budgetary dependence on tuition and fees grows, a drop in student enrollment becomes significant. Student fees represent, on average, over half of total revenue at private colleges, although smaller, modestly endowed private colleges often derive 90 percent or more of their revenue from this one source. Public institutions also are becoming dependent on student charges as state appropriations decline. Bond rating agencies deem student demand to be among the most critical factors in assessing creditworthiness, especially in schools with high tuition dependence.

Financial aid discounting often is closely linked to enrollment. CFOs should carefully examine not only how many students enroll but also how much financial aid was required to recruit them. Such aid is a discount against tuition and can offset in whole or in part any revenue gained from increased enrollment. Private institutions often lose a third or even a half of their tuition revenue to financial aid.

Comparative Perspective. Most of these data can be examined comparatively with a group of ten to twenty colleges or universities with whom the institution competes for students and faculty. The group should be as similar as possible to your own institution, particularly as to mission, student enrollment, budget, and endowment. Traditional competitors may not be truly comparable. A second comparison group may consist of "aspirational" colleges, i.e., institutions with which the college aspires to be comparable in the future.

Finding the right comparison group is tricky; other institutions must be true competitors and not just traditional rivals, and the group should be large enough (ten or more) to provide significant data and avoid the accounting differences that invalidate single institutional comparisons. For example, colleges inconsistently allocate fringe benefits as well as legal and technology expenses. Public colleges and universities often compare themselves with other institutions in their athletic conference or state system. The University of Massachusetts at Boston looks to the flagship campus at Amherst and other branches.

Although a comparison group is most useful for general perspective, institutions sometimes index parts of the budget to the group. Williams College aims to charge student fees at the median of competitor colleges. Allegheny, Sarah Lawrence, and other colleges set faculty salaries to maintain a certain position within their comparison groups. At Bowdoin, for example, we aim to pay faculty salaries at each rank at the seventy-fifth percentile or average of the fourth-, fifth-, and sixth-highest institutions within our eighteen-college comparison group (so we call the policy "4-5-6"). We also strive to increase student fees more slowly, as depicted in Figure 2.3. For example, from FY 1998 to FY 1999, Bowdoin's fees dropped from seventh highest among the eighteen-college group to tenth.

The same comparison group should be referenced for the entire budget. Comparing salaries against ten colleges and major maintenance against ten other colleges may be misleading. Each set of colleges may seek to be market leaders in that part of the budget, sometimes at the expense of other parts. Using a single comparison group ensures that the colleges and universities represented are making the same tough trade-offs between competing priorities (for example, salaries vs. major maintenance) that you are. (For a more complete discussion of comparator colleges or peer selection, see Chapter Twelve.)

The budget at Bowdoin College relies on institutional and comparative indicators that we did not define at the same time or very systematically. Slowly and inexorably, the trustees and administration defined new indicators over a 25-year period, as shown in Exhibit 2.2.

Figure 2.3. Comparative Student Fee Increases

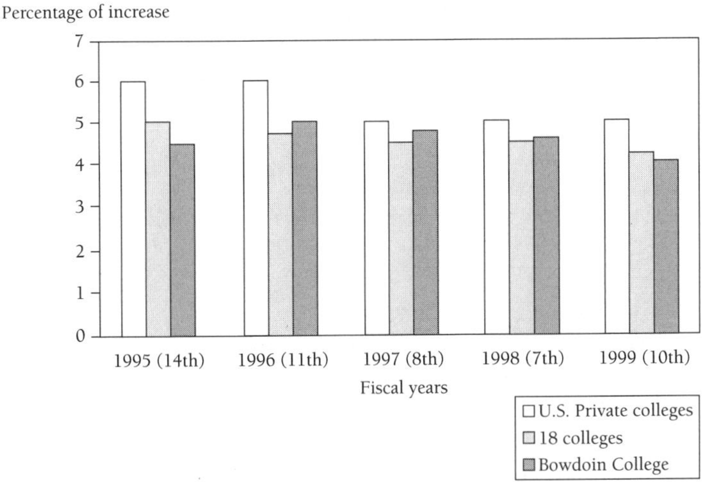

Percentage of increase

Fiscal years

□ U.S. Private colleges
□ 18 colleges
■ Bowdoin College

CFOs should ensure that indicators do not become too quantitative and drive the entire budget although that is what formula budgeting intends. Budgeting is not a mathematical exercise (if x, then y) but a very carefully prepared and debated policy process. Still, basing financial choices

Exhibit 2.2. Budget Indicators for Bowdoin College

Total budget: Balanced, with shifting emphasis toward academic programs and residential life and away from institutional support

Tuition and fees: Median of the eighteen-college comparison group

Financial aid: Need blind, spending between 12.5 to 14 percent of budget on 36 to 40 percent of students

Endowment spending: 4.75 percent long term of twelve-quarter lagging average of market value

Faculty salaries: "4-5-6" targets within the eighteen-college group, or seventy-fifth percentile

Administrative and support staff salaries: Fiftieth percentile of relevant labor markets

Employee benefits: Median of the eighteen-college group, or fiftieth percentile

Major maintenance and capital projects: $3 million, adjusted for inflation

Academic program: Achievement of 10.5:1 student-to-faculty ratio

Information technology: Four-year replacement cycle for desktop computers

Athletics: Median spending among athletic conference schools within four years

on strategic indicators has the paramount advantage of making the budget more predictable and relevant to the institution's most prized values and mission-centered programs.

References

Bryce, H. *The Nonprofit Board's Role in Establishing Financial Policies.* Washington, D.C.: National Center for Nonprofit Boards, 1996.
Chabotar, K. J. "Financial Ratio Analysis Comes to Nonprofits." *The Journal of Higher Education,* 1989, 60(2), 188–208.
Chabotar, K. J. "Managing Participative Budgeting in Higher Education." *Change,* 1995, 27(5), 21–29.
Chabotar, K. J., and Honana, J.P. *New Yardsticks to Measure Financial Distress.* Washington, D.C.: American Association for Higher Education, 1996.
Greene, D. (ed.). *College and University Business Administration.* (5th ed.) Washington D.C.: National Association of College and University Business Officers, 1992.
Herzlinger, R. E. "Effective Oversight: A Guide for Nonprofit Directors." *Harvard Business Review,* 1994, 72(4), 4–12.
Herzlinger, R. E., and Nitterhouse, D. *Financial Accounting and Managerial Control for Nonprofit Organizations.* Cincinnati: Southwestern Publishing, 1994.
Meisinger, R. J. *College and University Budgeting: An Introduction for Faculty and Academic Administrators.* (2nd ed.) Washington D.C.: National Association of College and University Business Officers, 1994.
Taylor, B. E., and others. "The New Work of the Nonprofit Board." *Harvard Business Review,* 1996, 74(5), 36–46.

KENT JOHN CHABOTAR *is vice president for finance and administration and treasurer at Bowdoin College and a member of the faculty of the Harvard Institutes for Higher Education.*

3

The pressure for cost containment is growing even at institutions that are financially very healthy. Institutions need to think concurrently about cost containment in terms of temporary, mid-term, and permanent changes to institutional operations and priorities.

The Thankless Task of Cost Containment

William S. Reed

Ask any chief financial officer (CFO) what makes him or her lose sleep at night, and you are likely to hear an impassioned story about cost containment. Regardless of the size, type, mission, or wealth of the school, the task of trying to reduce expenses is endemic to our industry. There are lots of reasons for this, and CFOs can rattle them off in what little sleep they can get: the pressure to restrain tuition increases; the public's concern about the cost of higher education; the growth in the need for financial aid and the corresponding reduction in the growth of net tuition; the potential of a paradigm shift in how education is delivered through distance learning; and the increased pressure to provide more technology in the classroom, just to name a few. What causes the loss of sleep is that the pressure to deal with the cost issue has grown in intensity during a period of extremely favorable economic conditions. What would happen if the stock market went into a sustained decline or if students began to opt for inexpensive degrees through distance learning?

The responsibility for dealing with the cost issue falls squarely on the shoulders of the CFO; this much is clear. What is not clear is where the authority resides to make the changes necessary to deal with the issue. The governance and organizational structures of most colleges and universities were not designed for efficiency. Colleges and universities are organized in a structure of departments and individuals that become spending machines. The irony is that the better the faculty, the greater the pressure on costs. Bright, dedicated faculty tend to generate creative ideas—new ways to teach, research to be undertaken, new courses to add to the curriculum, and emerging fields that need to be explored. Faculty members create a constant drumbeat to deliver and improve quality in the classroom, the research laboratory, the residence halls, the athletic fields, and every aspect of campus life.

There seems to be an infinite number of ideas on how to improve the educational product, but unfortunately there is a finite amount of money. The CFO has to produce a balanced budget, worry about long-term trends, talk reality to the board and the campus community, arbitrate between competing demands, get the most for every dollar spent, and figure out how to maintain morale while saying no. It is a challenging and, at times, thankless task.

In many respects the CFO becomes the messenger for the bad news. How the message is delivered is important, of course. Absent a crisis, the message has to be crafted carefully. When things are going well, the campus community assumes that if you just keep doing what you are doing, then things will continue to go well. When long-range projections show deficits down the road, the first response is to challenge the assumptions on which the projections were built. The second response is to argue that the problem is not one of expenditures but rather of an inability for revenues to grow quickly enough to keep pace with the growth in expenses. Simply put, the issue is redefined as a revenue problem, not an expense problem. With the careful presentation of data, appropriate benchmarks with peer institutions, and good, old-fashioned jawboning, the community will gradually accept the idea that something needs to change.

The hard work begins when the CFO, working with the cabinet or a budget advisory group, designs the process for deciding where to cut. In the ideal world, decisions on where to cut would be made rationally through a process that involves all elements of the community. In the real world of running a college, the hardest decisions are made by a handful of senior administrators. The CFO, through the budget document, delivers the news.

The Stages of Reducing Expenses

Depending on the severity of the cost pressures, there are three basic levels of dealing with reducing costs: temporary solutions, mid-term solutions, and permanent solutions. The CFO often will employ one or more of these solutions simultaneously.

Temporary Solutions. The budget-making process usually starts out with a deficit. Departmental requests will exceed the budget guidelines—new departmental initiatives will be proposed, requests for additional staff will be made, utility expenses will be inflated, or more computers will be requested than planned. During the routine budget-making process, most of these issues are dealt with, but a deficit may still remain. It is not unusual for the institution's fixed costs to consume all of the incremental revenue that is generated through projected increases in state appropriations, tuition increases, new gifts, and increased endowment support. The cost of salary increases, fringe benefits, financial aid, and inflationary adjustments to the nonpersonnel budgets of departments leaves very little, if anything, for innovation or new programs. In a typical college budget, no flexibility exists. High fixed costs take most of the incremental revenue. It is a game of running hard just to stay even. If, after all the arm wrestling with departments is over, there is still a deficit, a variety of temporary solutions may be employed:

- *Across-the-board cuts.* This is a mindless approach, but it works in the short term. All departments are requested to reduce their budgets by a set amount—say 3 percent. It is up to the department to determine how it will achieve savings. A fair amount of grumbling accompanies this approach, and some departments will have legitimate issues, which must be ignored lest one area appear to be favored over another.
- *Salary freezes.* In a typical operating budget, compensation accounts for 55 to 60 percent of expenses. Salaries are where the dollars are, and it is a logical place to start. Freezing salaries is never fun and cannot be done too often for obvious reasons. It can be employed to bring a budget into balance, but it does not address the long-term, systemic issues.
- *Freezing positions or openings.* Not filling open positions or putting a cap on the number of positions saves salary dollars. However, it adds a burden to the staff who must pick up the extra work. Without a restructuring of the workload, a hiring freeze is a temporary measure at best.
- *Temporarily cutting back on capital expenditures.* If the normal replacement cycle for desktop computers is every three years, it may be extended to four or five years. The purchase of scientific equipment may be delayed a year. This creates a backlog that sooner or later will have to be addressed.
- *Cutting back on major maintenance.* This approach, unfortunately, is common because it is easy to do. Delaying the replacement of a piece of equipment on a scheduled life cycle basis, postponing work on the electrical system, or not painting a building transfers an expense from one year to the next. These expenses must be made in the end. A year or two can be bought by extending the replacement cycle on equipment or by letting the campus deteriorate a little.

Mid-term Solutions. If the reality is that the budget pressures are more persistent than any of the temporary fixes listed above will address, a second level of measures are introduced. These measures begin to deal on the margin with structural issues. These are not radical measures, but they can have lasting, if modest, results.

- *Administrative process redesign.* When more permanent reductions are needed, administrative areas become likely candidates for consideration. The desire to find savings in administration is a natural and logical step because the administration is not the core of the enterprise. (No student enrolls at a college because the college has a terrific financial affairs office.) The process of finding savings usually takes the form of a study of administrative processes to see if steps can be eliminated and if the number of staff positions can be reduced.

Analyzing an administrative process is a fairly easy, if tedious, task. The hope is that the examination will show steps, procedures, or signatures that do not add value and can be eliminated. The objective is to create a more streamlined process that serves clients better, reduces bureaucracy, and makes better use of technology.

The question that has to be asked when one is going through a process redesign exercise is whether real savings will be realized or whether things will just become more efficient, with more time to do other things. It is difficult to eliminate whole positions in an administrative redesign because the redesigned process often occupies only a fraction of a staff member's time. What is most effective in the redesign of administrative processes is when departments are combined and staff positions reduced.

- *Business Process Reengineering (BPR).* Reengineering is a megaredesign process that is defined as the fundamental rethinking and radical redesign of business processes to bring about dramatic improvement in performance. A number of major research universities have undertaken significant reengineering efforts. The jury is still out. Most have reported major improvements in some of their business practices, but few have reported radical redesign or significant savings.

It is very difficult to realize radical redesign in a university setting. There is simply too much resistance to change; power and loyalty are dispersed in departments and sub-units. The organizational structure of a university is often described as loosely coupled. It is an axiom of reengineering that to be successful, the process must be driven from the topmost levels of an organization. That's the rub. It is difficult to get systemwide acceptance on anything, let alone a reengineering effort, in a loosely coupled structure.

In an article entitled "Challenges of Leading and Planning in Higher Education," the managerial problems associated with the loosely coupled structure of a university were elegantly summarized: In loosely coupled systems the forces for integration—for worrying about the whole, its identity, its integrity and its future—are often weak compared to the forces for specialization. Central authority, in important respects, is derived from the members rather than the member elements received delegated authority from above. The loosely coupled character of educational institutions requires a different approach to leading and planning.

Michael Hammer, the creator of the reengineering concept, believes that leadership from the top is essential to the successful implementation of a reengineering program. Put most simply, a leader is someone in a position to compel the compliance of all parties involved in reengineering. At the end of the day, if all else fails, the leader can simply demand that people contribute to the reengineering effort, that they subordinate their own domains to the needs of the new processes. Is it any wonder that reengineering efforts have had a rocky road in higher education? A president of a small college may have the authority envisioned by Mr. Hammer, but absent a crisis, she would not want to use one of her chips on a reengineering objective.

- *Outsourcing.* An important element in process redesign is a careful examination of whether a function can be outsourced to a third party. Outsourcing has the dual goal of increasing efficiency while reducing costs. With the growth in service providers to higher education, many administrative functions can be outsourced.

  Determining whether there will be true savings is not an easy calculation. A variety of variables have to be considered, not the least of which is the effect on staff morale and the political fallout. At Wellesley we studied the pros and cons of bringing in a third-party vendor to run our copy center. It was clear that substantial savings and service enhancements could be realized by outsourcing the copy center. I, naively, thought I was home free after I announced to Academic Council the impending change. The next day I knew I was in trouble when I saw a distinguished faculty member walking down the hall with a T-shirt that read "FRIEND OF THE COPY CENTER!"

- *Growth through substitution.* Because most colleges have a limit on the number of students they can accommodate, they cannot meet the growth in expenses or the addition of new programs by increasing student enrollment. In theory, to add a new program, an existing program should be eliminated. Many schools talk about practicing growth through substitution; my experience tells me that most have the growth part down pat but few have figured out how to drop a program. As much time should be spent on deciding what to drop as on what to add. It is difficult to discuss the substitution part of the equation, but the budgeting process must look at both sides of the equation if it is to keep in check the growth in embedded costs.

Permanent Changes. When the pressure to control cost reaches a point where something structural must be done, serious planning can begin. The smart CFO will not do the planning in isolation. A budget advisory committee or some multiconstituency committee should be engaged in the process.

The first step is to gather all of the facts that will be needed to make informed decisions. Gathering the financial facts can be accomplished by undertaking a benchmark study with peer institutions, which helps answer the first set of questions that will be asked by the advisory committee: Where are we out of line with our peers, and what areas have recently grown the most? Some schools go even further to develop internal data by undertaking an activity-based cost study. These studies provide detailed information on the cost of all major activities. An activity based accounting study is an enormous undertaking and should not be entered into lightly. It may be worth the effort, however. One important side benefit of such a study is that the campus community will awake to the cost of doing business. For many it is a real eye-opener. Armed with data about the cost of various activities, the advisory committee can begin to formulate an approach for a structural change that will contain costs.

No matter what, the advisory committee's recommendations will be controversial. Change does not come naturally or peacefully to an academic institution, especially permanent change in how programs are supported.

- *Expensive Policies.* An approach that is worthy of consideration because it helps to focus the discussion on policies, rather than on departments or individuals, is to examine the college's expensive policies. The phrase *expensive policies* can raise hackles with some, but its meaning is pretty clear.

   What are expensive policies? It's hard to answer because each institution has its own unique set. The point is to identify the expensive policies and then to ask these questions: Is this policy central to our mission? Is it an important institutional priority? Can it be changed?

   Without giving away confidential information about Wellesley, I will describe some of our expensive policies as a way to illustrate the point I am trying to make. The Budget Advisory Committee, working with the Budget Office, developed a comprehensive list of expensive policies. (Some members of the committee found the term *expensive policies* so offensive that they changed it to *valued policies.* I still prefer *expensive,* but I am a financial person.) The list was shared with the wider community, and so it grew. Students were particularly helpful in identifying what they consider expensive policies or practices. The following list includes some of Wellesley's expensive policies:

- Need-blind admissions and meeting the full needs of admitted students
- A student/faculty ratio of ten to one
- Budgeted enrollments of 2,180 to 2,190 that limit the number of first-year and transfer students when the campus could accommodate more students
- Dining halls in individual dorms
- Providing in-house services such as the Post Office and Printing Services
- No limit and expansion of students participating in foreign study and Twelve-College Exchange Programs
- Generous student support services
- Aggressive compensation objectives
- Annual salary increases for faculty and staff
- College calendar: Few students participating in winter session, few evening classes, low use classrooms during nonpeak hours.

- On-campus health service facilities
- A very high standard of building maintenance
- Commitment to providing juniors and seniors with single rooms
- Commitment to a multicultural campus, including student recruitment, faculty and staff hiring, and programming
- Commitment to maintain certain academic departments that have low enrollments
- Generous employee benefit plans, such as pension plans, college contribution to employee health insurance, and benefits available to part-time employees
- Strong commitment to technology in administration, classrooms, research laboratories, library, campus network, and associated training and programming
- Expansion of global outreach and programming

The list of expensive policies for Wellesley goes on for three pages and touches every aspect of the college. A frequently asked question is what makes a policy expensive? Can a policy that is very efficient, that costs less than at a peer institution, be considered expensive? The answer is yes. The issue is not efficiency but effectiveness. How important is the policy to the core mission of the college? That is the question that needs to be answered. Not everybody agrees, of course. But the discussion is focused on fundamental values and effectiveness of our policies. A change in any of the previously listed policies would be profound and would result in substantial cost savings.

The process of working through the expensive policies is time-consuming but highly instructive. The hard work is calculating the actual cost of the policy and weighing its value against that cost. Some policies do not need much discussion because they are so fundamental to the mission and culture of the college; others require a great deal of study and thought. It is hard to judge the impact of a change in policy, and care must be given to consider all of the consequences. In the end, few of the expensive policies will be changed, but some will, and others will be candidates for a second review if financial circumstances so dictate.

- *Draconian Cuts.* When the financial condition of a college is such that it has no choice but to drastically reduce costs, hard decisions are made quickly. It is a rare institution that makes the hard decisions absent a crisis. The manner in which these hard choices are made depends on the culture of the institution, the strength of the president, and the severity of the crisis.

Hard decisions involve reducing the payroll by eliminating positions and simultaneously eliminating functions, often referred to as rightsizing. To make the reductions in staff size permanent, attention has to be given to deciding what will no longer be done as well as the consequences. Careful planning is a must, and the positions to be eliminated cannot be voluntary. Early retirement programs do not work because the wrong people may leave. The focus has to be on deciding what work can be done without. Staff reduction programs must be accompanied by altering expectations of the service that used to be provided. If the expectation within the community is that the service will somehow still be provided, over time the positions will be added back.

Another approach is to eliminate programs or whole departments. This is the hardest type of decision to make, but it is the most permanent and the most effective. It takes a strong Provost, Dean, and President to drop an academic program or department. There are times when this approach is the only alternative. Such bold action can lead to a turnaround in the financial health of the institution. Northeastern University is an excellent example of how strong leadership and a willingness to drop programs, reduce staff, and shrink the size of the university led to a remarkable recovery of financial health.

Putting a Program Together

The question that must be addressed by the CFO is, what cost containment approach would be most effective in addressing the issues facing his or her institution? There is no right answer. Several approaches should be used at once. It makes sense to work on improving efficiency, eliminating redundant work, developing good benchmarks for comparison, and gathering data on areas that appear to be less efficient. It also makes sense to examine the institution's expensive policies so that the cost-benefit makeup of the policies is clearly understood. Adopting a single approach will probably not be enough. What is needed is a commitment to work on several fronts at once—along with the acceptance that providing quality education is expensive and that the pressure to contain cost will always be an issue for the CFO.

A Helpful Piece of Advice—Funding Priorities versus Cost Containment

Wellesley recently went through a reaccreditation process. As part of the self-study and discussion with the visiting team, a careful analysis was done of our efforts to constrain the rate of growth of our expenses. I lamented that I seemed to be talking about the issue all the time but nobody was listening. One of the members of the visiting team gave me an insight that was very helpful—and obvious. I was using the wrong words. People were tired of hearing about *cost containment*, especially when everything was going so well. She suggested I cease talking about cost containment and reframe the issue to one of *funding priorities*. People get excited about which priorities should be funded. There will be, of course, different opinions on what the priorities are. Discussing priorities should be a more effective way to engage the community in a thoughtful discussion of where we should invest and where we should cut back. This change of vocabulary should make the conversation more positive and engaging. No matter what, I am certain that in the years ahead keeping the cost of education within reasonable boundaries will be on every CFO's agenda.

WILLIAM S. REED is chief business officer at Wellesley College, Wellesley, Massachusetts.

4

The rapid advances in information technology (IT) have rendered conventional approaches to planning and budgeting for IT useless. What should a CFO think about in planning for the financial resources for campus IT needs?

Financial Planning for Information Technology: Conventional Approaches Need Not Apply

Ellen F. Falduto

"Roughly two decades after the first microcomputers arrived on college campuses, American colleges and universities experience computer and information technology (IT) planning as a continuing challenge. . . .just under half of U.S. colleges have a strategic plan for information technology. Concurrently, more than 60 percent do not have an IT financial plan." (Green, 1998, p. 3). Is it then any surprise that most colleges and universities cannot give accurate figures when asked what total institutional spending on information technology is (Green and Jenkins, 1998)?

Financial planning and budgeting for information technology are not easy tasks. Costs are not tracked easily because spending occurs within almost every departmental budget. Technology is the most rapidly changing support factor that higher education has yet experienced. In the 1980s mainframe systems had expected lives of five to seven years, but that has now been shortened to three. Microcomputers once resided in central common labs across campus; now nearly all faculty, staff, and students have personal computers and voice mail. Central data processing organizations used to handle much of an institution's administrative computing; now integrated systems proliferate end-user computing. A few technology-savvy faculty and senior staff had Bitnet addresses; now everyone has at least one e-mail address. Library shelves held reference materials; now libraries support electronic gateways to virtual reference materials. Institutions could rely on a few

NEW DIRECTIONS FOR HIGHER EDUCATION, no. 107, Fall 1999 © Jossey-Bass Publishers broadly trained computing staff to support all campus needs; now growing use and specialized technologies require more staff, that is, if funding is available to hire them.

The objective of this chapter is to provide chief financial officers with perspectives for developing an effective financial planning strategy for technology. The chapter will not prescribe the methodology for technology budgeting.

What Does Technology Really Cost?

Many surveys and estimates claim to report what technology really costs institutions. For example, the report of the 1998 Campus Computing Survey (Green, 1998) indicates that the average four-year private college spends $690,000 on academic computing and a total of $1.58 million on information technology. However, the survey does not answer this important question: What are the components of an institutional technology budget? Hartwick College, a four-year private, independent Baccalaureate I institution in rural upstate New York enrolling about fifteen hundred full-time residential students, serves as an example of what is included. The college provides every student with a notebook computer, printer, software, network access, telephone, voice mail, Web page space, e-mail, and video broadcast services. The technology budget is funded by student fees and other revenues and includes annual and capital expenses accounting for approximately 7 percent of the college's total operating budget. The components offered by Hartwick College are typical of the breadth and variety of services and programs found at colleges and universities.

How Do We Budget for Technology?

The strategies that colleges and universities employ to budget for information technology include traditional departmentally based or cost-center budgets, one-time funding allocations, user fees, and chargebacks. Institutions fund the increasing costs of technology by fees, obtaining outside grants for specific projects, recycling older equipment, reorganizing operations, using technology to reduce instructional costs, and using student assistants to meet growing user support demands (Green, 1998). Interestingly, these strategies have not changed significantly in the last decade, despite the growing use and demand for technology and related services on campus.

The degree to which institutions have adopted funding strategies mirrors institutional culture; for example, more universities and research institutions charge fees for e-mail and Internet access than do private two- and four-year institutions; student technology fees and chargebacks characterize public institutions more than private ones (Green, 1998). Technology budgeting and cost management strategies reflect broader institutional budgeting and resource allocation philosophies.

There have been many attempts to determine the "total cost of owner-ship" of technology. Most efforts to date, including those widely published or quoted in business and technology presses, are "mystifying" (Leach and Smallen, 1998, p. 38). The difficulty arises from the lack of comparability among institutions in accounting methods. One objective of Leach and Smallen's project (1998) was to provide reliable and consistent cost bench-marking data for typical technology functions and services for higher edu-cation institutions.

The current financial planning landscape for information technology can be characterized as one where financial planning is an adaptation of existing budgeting processes. The problem with this approach is in the assumption that the technology landscape serenely rolls along. The land-scape is shifting, and the underpinnings of technology infrastructures require redesign to support future efforts.

Shifts in the Landscape: For What Are We Planning?

A 1986 survey of colleges indicated that microcomputers were an "emerg-ing area" in higher education "that has developed faster than expected and with which existing planning mechanisms have been unable to cope." (Fer-rante, Hayman, Carlson, and Phillips, 1986, p. 42). Nearly fifteen years later, higher education remains unable to cope. The microcomputer is no longer emerging but rather is the primary force for change in the demand for tech-nology tools and services. Figure 4.1 illustrates some of the shifts in the technology landscape since the 1980s when most technology budgeting strategies were adopted.

Shift 1: Thinking. In the 1980s higher education was admonished to begin thinking about PCs as capital (Weisman, 1989); today, a PC costs about $1,200 per desktop, has a useful life of three years or less, and is thought of as disposable. Colleges and universities once purchased large mainframe systems that served the institution for five to seven years; today colleges purchase multiple desktop-size servers to support applications for the period of their warranties. Support staff distributed throughout campus replaced centralized academic and administrative technology operations to promote end-user computing rather than centralized data processing. Today, technology is considered a "strategic resource" instead of a research tool for faculty and students in the sciences and quantitative areas of the social sci-ences (Detweiler, 1996; Dolence and Norris, 1995; Katz and Associates, 1999). Technology is essential and pervasive. The management of technol-ogy no longer succeeds by using traditional management and human resource policies; new management strategies and creative human resource policies are required to attract and retain information technology profes-sionals.

Purchasing versus Leasing. In the 1980s and early 1990s colleges and universities purchased rather than leased technology. At that time, this

Figure 4.1. Shifts in Thinking About Institutional Technology

Then (1980s)	→	Now (1999)
Capital	→	Disposable
One or more big systems	→	Several small systems
Specialized equipment	→	No special equipment
Research tool	→	Strategic resource
Centralized computing	→	End-user computing
Work-Day computing	→	"24 × 7 × 365" computing
Traditional human resource policies	→	New management and human resource strategies
Purchase	→	Lease
Budget or reserve finance	→	Debt financing
Expense	→	Revenue opportunity
In-House development and support projects	→	Outsource; special/one-time

approach posed no problem for technology acquisition, but in 1999 leasing deserves a close second look. With institutions acquiring more systems with warranties that approximate their useful lives, leasing becomes a more attractive option because interest rates and returns on investment portfolios are much higher than the cost of leasing. Leasing enables institutions to establish smaller constant budgets for systems rather than try to plan for one-time funding allocations for replacement every three years.

Several institutions have adopted lease programs to acquire student-used notebook computers with "technology refresh options" (that is, students' computers are automatically upgraded at the end of their second year). Leasing for the first two years guarantees return of the notebooks rather than the college having to resell and may provide better warranty coverage. Some caveats: vendor leasing programs vary widely in their terms and costs. Third-party leasing may be more economical and should not impact the vendor's warranty support provisions. Leasing can significantly increase the expense of pervasive computer programs, such as notebook programs, because cost per student may be nearly three times what it would cost to purchase the systems outright. If an institution is considering a notebook program, various combinations of lease and purchase should be analyzed, especially if the plan is to have the students own the notebook upon graduation.

Debt Financing. Many institutions require campus infrastructure upgrades (ranging from network wiring and reconfiguring traditional classrooms into multimedia teaching spaces to acquisition of satellite dish farms) in addition to hardware and software upgrades. One strategy is to use debt financing for projects such as similar-scale facilities upgrades. If possible, the ideal is to accomplish these upgrades in conjunction with planned facilities modernization.

Outsourcing versus Working In-House. Many colleges currently outsource services such as configuration of notebook PCs each summer for new students and faculty, long-distance telephone resale accounting, and all programming for administrative applications. However, there are two fundamental issues with outsourcing. The first is the presumption that outsourcing is more expensive than working in-house. Certainly, if an institution outsources all of its technology operations, doing so will be more expensive, for the firms that provide these services need to cover their overhead and make a profit. However, it is often more cost effective to outsource one-time or infrequent activities (such as system conversions, mass PC configurations, or installation of new hardware). If the college does not have or does not want or need to acquire and maintain the staff resources to provide a service (such as billing and accounting operations for telephone resale services or programming for administrative computing systems), outsourcing may be a better option.

The second issue is staff fear of job loss because of outsourcing. Assuming all else is equal, that staff are competent, that the technology staff has more than enough work to do, and that the institution finds it difficult to find technology staff when the need arises, outsourcing may be the optimal strategy. The college can purchase expertise to assist and support staff rather than replace them. The quickest way for a CFO to alienate the institution's technology staff and chief information officer (CIO) is to declare naïvely that the institution will look at outsourcing technology operations.

Shift 2: Components of the Technology Budget. In the 1980s technology budgets were relatively simple. Centralized academic and administrative computing departments had staff, hardware maintenance, occasional software, supplies, and costs to time-share on larger, regional computers. Hardware was purchased periodically (mainframes were purchased approximately every seven to ten years) and hardware upgrades to these systems were funded when needed, when funds could be allocated, or in the case of emergencies. The same was true for most major software packages that ran on mainframes.

Year 2000 (or Y2K) technology budgets are more complex, resulting from changes in technology and the pervasiveness of information technology. A typical technology budget is organized around curricular technology, video services, media services, user support services, telecommunications, networking, information services, and occasionally research and development. The simplicity of relying on academic use and administrative use as organizing principles for technology budgets no longer suffices, although many organizational structures continue to reflect this model. Revenues from student and user fees and sales of services fund increasing expenditures for staff; annual purchases of hardware or leases of systems; software licenses; support services, including training programs; technology services, including Internet and video service providers; supplies; repair parts; professional development for staff; and infrastructure and facilities upgrades.

Where once institutions could budget every so many years for hardware and infrastructure upgrades, upgrades now are required annually.

Shift 3: Useful Lives. Hardware is now relatively disposable; software changes every six to twelve months. Facilities used to require little change to support technology operations because basements were ideal spaces for heavy computing equipment that required refrigerator-like environmental conditions. Now main systems are office-environment ready and staff must be accessible to users. Knowledge required of technology staff was relatively stable; now the demand for staff with specialized knowledge exceeds the supply, driving up salaries and increasing professional development budgets. The rapid changes in technology increased the demand for support staff and hours of service, primarily in help desk roles, and spawned technology research and development offices that have responsibility to investigate and create prototypes for emerging technologies and applications.

Shift 4: Technology Does Not Save Money. Despite the transformationists' argument that technology would result in cost savings from increased productivity (Dolence and Norris, 1995), little, if any, definitive data demonstrate whether technology implementations save or reduce costs (Detweiler, 1996). What happens is substitution. Technology may reduce the cost of an old process, it may make work simpler and provide less time-on-old-task for faculty and staff, but the money and time saved is used to support the cost of technology or to do other things. Technology provides the ability to substitute resources, streamline processes, and support more complex functions.

The New Financial Planning and Budgeting Paradigm

The key to a good financial and budgeting plan is simplicity (Ringle, 1997). No matter how sophisticated the technology program and infrastructure, no matter how complex the organization, no matter how idiosyncratic the institution's budgeting and accounting processes, a successful financial plan and budgeting program for information technology comes down to a few basics.

Get a Technology Plan. The basis of a financial plan for information technology is the institutional strategic plan, because technology, like academic programs, student services, and facilities, is funded from institutional resources. It has been more than a decade since higher education was first advised to plan for information technology, yet today more than one-half of colleges do not have a plan for technology (Green, 1998).

Most institutions have an institutional plan. At the very least, the plans are ceremonial documents that demonstrate the existence of a plan to outside funders. At the other extreme, plans are agile documents that guide every action of an institution and provide accountability benchmarks against which the institution measures its progress. The challenge is to develop a technology plan that comports with the institutional plan, making it possible to evaluate priorities for resource allocation within a holistic context. Some institutions have leveraged their technology plan to advance their institutional plan (Detweiler, 1996).

Develop the Institutional Financial Plan. The development of an institutional financial plan for technology has two components: the mechanics of budget modeling, and the art of communication.

The Mechanics of the Financial Plan. The financial plan for technology should cover at least seven years, knowing that after the third year, the probability is low that what had originally been envisioned will be implemented. Given this, the financial plan for technology must be updated at least annually.

Organize the plan around technology goals. Hartwick College's budget organization reflects the various major programs defined in the college's technology plan. Annual budget allocations to each component vary based on the goals (projects) outlined in the technology plan.

The components of the financial plan will vary depending on the scope of the technology plan and the institution. For example, the financial plan for a residential institution with ubiquitous computing and networking programs will be different from that of a primarily commuter institution that opts to leverage its technology investment to support nontraditional and distance learning programs. The basic components of the financial plan for technology include the familiar categories of revenues and expenses. Funding sources for the former include fees charged to students, fees collected for resale of technology products and services, cash fees charged to other users for services, and new revenues from new programs possible from the investments in technology. Conversely, all of the typical budget categories for expenses apply to technology. Given the dynamics of technology and institutions' needs to attract and retain competent technology staff, investment in staffing is as critical as investments for the technology itself. Often professional development opportunities are not available within the local area, necessitating additional expenditures for travel.

Technology-specific expenses include hardware, software, and services. Hardware may or may not be a capital expense depending on the equipment and the means of financing. If equipment is leased, it may be reflected as an annual operating expense; if it is purchased, it is reflected as a periodic capital expense. The determination is best made by considering the expected useful life of the hardware; both budgeting for leases and capital acquisition reflect life cycle budgeting strategies. Software should be budgeted annually. Typical software acquired by colleges and universities is either purchased on an annual renewable license basis or purchased as a perpetual license, usually as a one-time expense with an annual fee for maintenance. The exception to this is software for major institution-wide applications such as library systems, administrative systems, building management, and retail systems. These are usually purchased with a one-time acquisition fee of several thousand dollars and are intended to serve the institution for several years. As such, these should be budgeted as capital acquisitions, though there is typically an annual maintenance and support fee for such systems.

Services are a relatively new category of technology expense and include annual expenditures for Internet access, video broadcast feeds from cable and satellite providers, and trunk access to local and long-distance telephone service providers.

The financial plan for technology will include new revenues, expenses, and existing resources. Existing resources allocated to technology are considered recyclables. With rapid changes in technology and applications, technology operations are always in flux and more likely to be replacing old activities with new ones. Funds that were supporting annual maintenance contracts on large mainframe systems can be shifted to leasing servers when it comes time to replace the mainframe. Staff who were programming report-generator applications in support of an in-house administrative computing system can support users in developing queries on a new vendor-provided integrated information system. Budgets for mainframe software licenses can underwrite the cost of individual licenses for the PC version of the same software. Student employment and work-study funds that paid students who had generic jobs supporting labs and various computing operations can leverage new structures for more effectively engaging students in supporting the technology enterprise and addressing the growing needs of all users.

The decision as to whether to use chargebacks is a philosophical one. For institutions whose operating philosophy and culture are based in unit or school independence (the "every tub on its own bottom" concept), chargebacks are the means of allocating central technology expenses to each unit in addition to technology expenses funded within the unit's own budget. This is typically the strategy at large research and state institutions. For small institutions, an elaborate system of chargebacks may be counterproductive to what the institution is attempting to achieve through technology. Many departments do not have sufficient resources to pay the real costs of technology and are dependent on the general institutional budget for the tools and access to technology resources. Chargebacks to departments do not provide any new resources for technology; institutions either can fund technology as technology or fund departments for technology. Either way, the resources will need to be found.

Avoid one-time funding allocations. The best use for these is a pilot program or released time for faculty to work on curricular redesign using technology. This opens up more opportunities to seek other sources such as research grants, foundation support, faculty development funding, institutionally funded research grants for faculty, corporate support, and specifically targeted gifts.

The Art of Communication. The responsibility for the institutional financial plan does not rest solely with the CFO; in fact, the chief technology officer and technology advocates bear just as much responsibility for this as the CFO. If technology is competing for limited institutional resources, it is incumbent on technology advocates to educate senior officers on the technology plan and how the plan will advance broader institutional goals. If implementing the technology plan requires new resources or reallocation of existing resources from outside the technology budget, this must be communicated clearly to faculty, students, staff, and governing board members. Benefits of implementing the technology plan must be clearly understood and endorsed by the campus community.

Collaborate with Your CIO. A CFO must understand the technology marketplace (Green and Jenkins, 1998). As rapidly as technology changes, there is no promise that this article will be current when you read this! Therefore, it is important that the CFO understand the issues from a variety of perspectives: chief academic officers look at technology, curriculum, teaching, and faculty impacts; student life officers consider the impact of technology and access to the Internet on students developmentally; admissions officers look at how technology can be leveraged to recruit and retain the right students for the institution; advancement officers rely on technology for maintaining sophisticated prospect information systems and communicating with internal and external publics using emerging web-based media; governing boards grapple with the issues of technology within the framework of their individual experiences in corporations, agencies, and other educational institutions; and students want access to technology for educational and entertainment purposes. Presidents care about all of these issues as well as the financial impacts. Your institution's chief technology officer should be well aware of all the various stakeholders' perspectives and possess the understanding of the technology landscape while carrying the headaches of making it all work. Talk with your CIO often.

Reach Beyond the Conventional. The 1998 Campus Computing Survey (Green, 1998) indicated that when it comes to managing technology costs and identifying resources for technology funding, most institutions continue to utilize conventional approaches. To respond to growing technology needs, agility in budgeting and financing processes is required (see Table 4.1).

Options beyond the conventional exist. Some of these are considered opportunistic, being responses or reactions to new funding sources and to reallocation of current resources. For example, new or increased fees can support new programs, especially ones that give students equipment to use or network services. New approaches to managing technology, for instance, campus technology standards, enable the institution to negotiate volume pricing, provide a common hardware and software platform that is more easily supported by technology staff, and enable users to informally help one another.

Another example is the "90-90" rule (Detweiler, 1996), which advocates meeting 90 percent of user needs 90 percent of the time by establishing institution-wide goals for technology services based on the most frequent and typical uses while providing special sites for advanced needs.

Table 4.1. Approaches to Technology Budgeting and Financing

Conventional	Opportunistic	Entrepreneurial
One-time funding acquisition	One-time funding for pilot and curriculum development	
As-needed replacement	Life cycle funding	
Central technology budgets	Program-based budgets	Profit and loss center
Purchase	Lease	
Cost recovery/chargeback		Internal lease programs
Student/user fees	Student fees for new tangible services	Revenues from new programs
Consortia purchasing	Campus technology standards	
Reduce PC purchases	Mandatory ownership programs	
Recycle old equipment		Resale of aging equipment before it gets too old
Reduce services	Substitute services	Expand services through new ventures
In-house services	Selected outsourced services	
Student workers	Student technology assistants	Paid internships with fee to corporations to support program administration

Requiring all students to purchase notebook computers not only is a means for generating revenue to support technology operations but is also likely to reduce reliance on central computer labs and the costs associated with their upkeep and management.

Other strategies are considered entrepreneurial. Once the technology infrastructure is in place, new programs or services can be provided to generate new revenues. In addition to educational and professional development programs, institutions can reach beyond their campus boundaries and provide services to the local community. Programs can be developed that enable departments to gradually build budgets to support their technology needs.

Both the opportunistic and entrepreneurial approaches are leaps of faith. Given the dynamic nature of technology, the circumstantial evidence of the promise of technology to transform educational institutions, the unproven promises of cost reductions attributable to technology implementations, and the uncertainty of what the technological future holds, investments in technology are somewhat of a gamble. Conley (in Detweiler, Falduto, Conley, and Golden, 1996) argues "Everything worthwhile in life (choosing an education, getting married, having children, starting a business, obtaining heaven) is a leap of faith. Those who don't leap become 'leapt-overs.'"

Monitor Plan Progress. The technology planning and budgeting processes do not end with the adoption of the financial plan. Progress on technology efforts, financial plan assumptions, and outcomes must be monitored. Monitoring plan progress is essential for effective management of technology programs and for alleviating the fears and skepticism associated with large investments in technology. Periodic reporting on expenditures, implementation status, services, user satisfaction with technology services, and educational and operational outcomes is good assessment practice. This information also informs the ongoing refinement of the technology plan and financial plan.

What Is in IT for a CFO?

In financial planning and budgeting for technology, a CFO participates in planning for the force that has the greatest potential to transform higher education. There are immediate and direct benefits of interest to CFOs, including appropriate technology systems to support financial tracking and reporting systems, potential for electronic business transactions, campus card systems, and executive information systems that provide senior administrators with access to key institutional information. There are potential benefits of new educational programs and new means of delivering instruction that can bring new students to the institution, thus enhancing the revenue stream to pay for the investment in technology (Dolence and Norris, 1995). The most significant benefit is that the institution will have both a plan and financial model for its technology investments. The CFO will also have an understanding of the importance of technology to the institution, an understanding of the components of the cost of technology, and knowledge of what technology costs the institution.

Conclusion

Financial planning and budgeting for information is a fusion of art and science. There is no one way to plan or budget for technology. The most successful efforts are consistent with the institution's overall plan, efforts that recognize the constantly changing landscape of information technology and the challenges that this discipline presents. The resulting financial planning and budgeting approaches reflect conventional, opportunistic, and entrepreneurial approaches. CFOs must muster their financial planning and communications skills, be agile in approach, and be willing to take the leap of faith required to develop and endorse the financial planning and accounting models essential to support their institution's information technology efforts.

References

Detweiler, R. A. "Mission: Ubiquity." *Trusteeship*, 1996, special issue, pp. 20–25.
Detweiler, R. A., Falduto, E. F., Conley, D. B., and Golden, R. M. "IT's in the Plan! — Integrating Institutional and IT Planning." Paper presented at CAUSE96, San Francisco, December 1996.
Dolence, M. G., and Norris, D. M. *Transforming Higher Education: A Vision for Learning in the 21st Century.* Ann Arbor: Society for College and University Planning, 1995.
Ferrante, R., Hayman, J. Jr., Carlson, M. S., and Phillips, H. *Planning for Microcomputers in Higher Education: Strategies for the Next Generation.* ASHE-ERIC Higher Education Report, no. 7. Washington, D.C.: Association for the Study of Higher Education, 1988.
Green, K. C. *Campus Computing 1998: The Ninth National Survey of Desktop Computing and Information Technology in Higher Education.* Encino, Calif.: Campus Computing, 1998.
Green, K., and Jenkins, R. "IT Financial Planning 101." *NACUBO Business Officer*, 1998, 31(9), 32–37.
Katz, R. N., and Associates. *Dancing with the Devil: Information Technology and the new Competition in Higher Education.* San Francisco: Jossey-Bass, 1999.
Leach, K., and Smallen, D. "What Do Information Technology Support Services Really Cost?" *CAUSE/EFFECT*, 1998, 21(2), 38–45.
Ringle, M. D. "Forecasting Financial Priorities for Technology." *CAUSE/EFFECT*, 1997, 20(3), 22–29.
Weissman, R. F. E. "Capital Budgeting and Lifecycle Planning for Desktop Technology." In B. L. Hawkins (ed.), *Organizing and Managing Information Resources on Campus.* Washington, D.C.: EDUCOM, 1989.

ELLEN F. FALDUTO *is chief information and planning officer at Hartwick College, Oneonta, New York. She previously served as university budget director and assistant to the executive vice president at Drew University, New Jersey.*

5

The endowment contributes to the financial stability of an institution and provides a funding source for important initiatives. This chapter describes the critical policy decisions that must be made by the CFO and the board investment or finance committee.

Investment Policies for College and University Endowments

William T. Spitz

Kingman Brewster, the former president of Yale, has pointed out that colleges have three endowments: the intellectual capital vested in the faculty, the physical plant, and the investment portfolio. This chapter focuses on management of the financial endowment with particular emphasis on critical investment policy decisions. As it turns out, these policies largely determine the success of the endowment because they overwhelm the impact of tactical investment decisions such as the selection of individual securities. This conclusion suggests that financial officers and governing boards should devote the majority of their time to establishing and reviewing investment policy rather than the selection of investment managers.

A Perpetual Fund

Webster's Dictionary defines an *endowment* as a "perpetual fund, the income from which is used to support a particular program or purpose." Although simple and straightforward, this definition has important implications for endowment management. First, the support provided by the endowment is a critical component of the budget for many institutions. Therefore, investment policies must be designed to provide reasonable growth and predictability of the annual endowment payout. Second, the perpetual nature of the fund provides both opportunities and challenges. The opportunity lies in the ability to commit to complex, illiquid, or long-term investments that can reasonably be expected to generate superior returns. The challenge results from the fact that most individuals have a difficult time expanding their time horizon beyond the term of their position or service on the investment committee. Therefore, many endowments are governed in accordance with a 3- to- 5-year time horizon rather than a 50- or 100-year period that would be more consistent with the true life of the institution. Successful endowment management represents the achievement of a balance between the current needs of the institution and the perpetual nature of the fund.

The Fundamental Goals of Endowment Management

The most basic fiduciary responsibility of an endowment trustee is preservation of the corpus of the fund in perpetuity. Historically, this responsibility was interpreted as the preservation of the *original* value of the corpus, which typically resulted in large allocations to bonds, cash equivalents, and other low risk investments. Two events led to a revision in the generally accepted standard of fiduciary responsibility. First, the average endowment lost approximately 60 percent of its purchasing power during the decade of the 1970s owing to a combination of high inflation and low investment returns. Second, a majority of the U.S. states passed the Institutional Management of Funds Act, which specifically requires trustees to consider the impact of inflation.

Today, knowledgeable trustees interpret their minimum responsibility as the preservation of the real or inflation-adjusted value of both the endowment fund and the annual transfer to the operating budget. In other words, an endowment with an initial value of $1,000,000 must grow to $1,030,000 after one year, assuming 3 percent inflation. Similarly, the annual transfer from the endowment to the operating budget would have to increase to $51,500, assuming that $50,000 was spent during the prior year. Otherwise, the institution experiences a declining level of support from the endowment fund. More broadly, this concept is known as *generational equity*, which suggests that future generations of endowment beneficiaries must be provided with at least the same level of support that current beneficiaries enjoy. This goal has been easy to achieve during the bull markets of the 1980s and 1990s, but trustees and financial officers should not be lulled into complacency because there have been many periods when preservation of real value was illusive.

Sustainable Spending

The necessity to preserve the real value of both the corpus and the annual endowment payout dictates the prudent level of annual spending. Specifically, the sustainable spending rate is equal to the expected total return on the endowment less the projected inflation rate. For example, a fund that generates an average total return of 9 percent can transfer 5 percent of its value to the operating budget each year, assuming a 4 percent inflation rate.

In this case, return equal to 4 percent is reinvested in the corpus, which exactly offsets the loss in purchasing power attributable to inflation.

Although simple enough, this formula actually requires the trustees to agree on several difficult forecasts. First, they must make an assumption regarding future inflation. A simple approach is to extrapolate historical data for a readily available measure of inflation such as the consumer price index (CPI)but this method may not be adequate because budgets of educational institutions typically grow at a rate that exceeds the CPI by approximately 1 percent per annum. The ideal measure of inflation is the predicted growth in the budget of each particular institution. One side benefit of using this measure is that it stimulates a discussion between the governing board and management regarding future trends in key financial variables. For those who prefer to use a standardized benchmark, the higher education price index (HEPI) represents a reasonable alternative because it is designed to closely replicate the operating budget of an educational institution. Second, the trustees must agree on a reasonable assumption regarding the total return that will be generated by the endowment fund. This topic will be covered in the next section of this chapter.

Once agreement is reached on the appropriate level of spending, many institutions choose to implement a spending formula because strict adherence to the formula eliminates the temptation to (supposedly) temporarily increase spending to meet pressing budget needs. Although these formulas are customized to meet the needs of each institution, most represent a variant of one of three basic models. First, a small percentage of colleges and universities spend *annual income,* defined as dividends and interest received. A more popular alternative calls for spending a percentage of the market value of the fund. This total-return approach is often based on a moving average of market value to smooth out annual fluctuations that would otherwise wreak havoc on the budgeting process. For example, a very popular formula calls for spending 5 percent of the average value of the endowment during the three prior fiscal years. Finally, some institutions increase the prior year's spending in dollars by the rate of inflation, which results in a highly predictable flow of income to the operating budget.

Each of these approaches has important drawbacks. In today's environment of low dividend yields and interest rates, the income-only rule is likely to result in spending of only 2.5 percent or so. On a longer-term basis, this rule leads to a preference for bonds and other securities with high current yields, which is likely to diminish the total return on the endowment. A policy of automatically increasing annual spending can result in erosion of the corpus during a sustained bear market. And even with a smoothing mechanism, the total-return policy generates some volatility in the annual payout. In the final analysis, selecting among these alternatives boils down to a decision as to whether the institution can better tolerate volatility in the corpus or the spending stream.

The Relationship Between Asset Allocation and Spending

As previously mentioned, the sustainable level of spending is determined by the projected return on the endowment, given an inflation assumption. In turn, its asset mix largely determines the return on a diversified fund. A number of studies have found that market timing and security selection account for less than 10 percent of the variation in return from one fund to the next. More than 90 percent of the variation is a function of the relative weighting in stocks, bonds, cash, real estate, and other asset classes. Because asset allocation determines return, the asset mix and spending rate must be consistent with one another.

Trustees and CFOs can approach the spending and asset allocation decisions from either direction. For example, an institution might select a high level of spending, which would then require a relatively aggressive asset mix. (Generally, this would mean a high level of exposure to equities.) On the other hand, the investment committee might reasonably conclude that it has a low level of tolerance for volatility or risk in the portfolio, which would lead it to allocate a modest portion of the fund to equities. This decision would result in a lower projected return on the portfolio, which reduces the sustainable level of spending.

To illustrate these concepts, it is instructive to analyze the asset allocation and spending rate of the average endowment fund for fiscal 1997. According to the NACUBO endowment study, a simplified portfolio breakdown of the average endowment was as shown in Table 5.1. We will assume that the categories shown in Table 5.1 earn future total returns of 11 percent, 6 percent, and 4 percent, respectively, which approximate the actual return on marketable securities during this century. The product of the projected returns and the portfolio weights is 9.4 percent, which is a simple estimate of the potential return on the average fund. In reality, the actual return is likely to be modestly higher because the equity category includes categories such as private equity, which should outperform marketable securities. Adjusting for this factor, a more realistic return forecast might be 9.8 percent. Consumer price inflation has averaged 3.2 percent during this century, which suggests a 4.2 percent average increase in educational budgets, assuming that higher education budgets continue to increase at a rate that is 1 percent greater than inflation, the historical spread. Combing the return and inflation forecasts, a spending rate of about 5.6 percent (9.8−4.2) therefore seems sustainable. In fact, the average endowment spent 5.7 percent during fiscal 1997, which indicates that trustees are acting in a responsible manner. (The cost of managing the fund is included in the 5.7 percent.)

The cost of a mismatch between spending and asset allocation can be very serious. For example, assume that an institution has a relatively high spending rate of 6 percent and a relatively conservative asset mix of 50 percent stocks and 50 percent bonds. Using the same assumptions as in the

**Table 5.1. Simplified Portfolio
Breakdown of Average Endowment**

	Portfolio (%)
Equities (broadly defined)	70
Fixed-income securities	25
Cash equivalents	5
Total Fund	100

previous analysis, this fund can expect to earn a return of 8.5 percent, which is reduced by the 6 percent payout. Therefore, it is reinvesting 2.5 percent in the corpus, which lags the expected rate of inflation of 4.2 percent by 1.7 percent per annum. At the end of fifty years, this inadequate level of reinvestment results in a 57 percent decline in the purchasing power of the corpus.

The Asset Allocation Decision

The asset allocation decision should be based on a blend of sophisticated financial analysis, evaluation of the practices of similar institutions, and a heavy dose of judgment and common sense. As was illustrated previously, a reasonable starting point involves calculating the minimum level of equity exposure necessary to generate sufficient return to sustain the institution's spending rate. For example, a 5 percent spending rate requires equity exposure of at least 65 percent based on the assumptions just listed. Although this simple analysis provides useful information, most institutions will want to engage in a more sophisticated asset allocation study. First, the simple calculation considers only two asset classes, whereas most institutions invest in a number of traditional and alternative categories. Second, this simple approach does not provide any information regarding the amount of risk inherent in a given mix.

Two computer-based tools are available to help trustees and financial officers construct a portfolio structure that is likely to meet their needs. First, an *optimizer* identifies the asset mix that delivers the highest projected return for a given level of risk as measured by the standard deviation of return. The output of an optimization analysis generally includes suggested portfolio structures for a range of risk levels. Second, a *simulation package* depicts the likely behavior of a portfolio structure that is defined by the user. The simulation provides information on the probability of achieving various return objectives and the magnitude of potential losses. Many institutions rely on the optimizer to identify a potential asset mix and then use the simulation program to evaluate the probability that the chosen mix will achieve its goals.

Although these are useful tools, it is important to understand their limitations. First, they are usually based on simple extrapolation of historical returns, standard deviations, and correlations for each asset class, and modest changes in the assumptions can meaningfully impact the recommended portfolio. Second, although they provide an indication of the amount of risk inherent in a given asset mix, they do not absolve the trustees from the responsibility of selecting the appropriate level of risk for the institution.

The actual process followed by many institutions begins with the selection of a tentative asset mix based on one of these computerized tools or a combination of them. This mix is then compared with those of similar institutions and subjected to discussion by the trustee committee. The weightings are often adjusted to make the structure more traditional and palatable to each of the institution's constituencies. The final asset mix represents the strategic or equilibrium structure of the portfolio. Most institutions develop a policy on rebalancing to ensure that the actual weightings do not drift too far from the targets, and some choose to select both a target weight and a range of acceptable portfolio weights for each category to allow for a modest degree of tactical asset allocation.

There are no hard and fast rules as to how often this process should be repeated, but it is common practice to conduct an asset allocation study every five years or whenever there has been a significant shift in the financial status of the institution. A more difficult challenge is deciding whether it is appropriate to update return assumptions on the basis of recent returns that are very different from long-term averages. Have the financial markets changed or does recent experience simply represent an aberration?

The Role of Alternative Assets

In addition to their allocation to traditional securities such as domestic stocks and bonds, most institutions now have at least some exposure to foreign securities, real estate, private equity, and other so-called alternative assets. The current rush into these categories may well represent a fad of sorts, but there are very compelling fundamental reasons to consider adding these asset classes to an endowment portfolio.

First, nontraditional categories tend to have low or even negative correlation with stocks and bonds, which means that their inclusion in the portfolio will dampen its volatility. More important, many alternative assets can be expected to generate superior returns. Economics teaches that an investor should expect to earn a liquidity premium by committing to investments that are not readily marketable. Given the perpetual nature of an endowment, why not attempt to earn that premium on a portion of the fund? Second, both theory and empirical data suggest that private markets are less efficient than public markets, which should provide a skilled investor with the opportunity to significantly outperform his or her competition.

Nontraditional investments also have important drawbacks. Obviously, many of these investments are illiquid, but this should not pose a problem for a portion of a perpetual fund. Second, the selection of alternative investments entails intensive analysis and specialized expertise. Finally, nonmarketable investments pose a number of accounting, valuation, and performance measurement challenges. Fortunately, even those institutions with modest investment offices can overcome these drawbacks by using funds of funds and other commingled vehicles.

The Optimal Use of Committee Time

Even though research demonstrates that the return on a fund is largely determined by its asset mix, many investment committees devote relatively little time to this subject. Instead, they spend a great deal of time selecting investment managers and listening to presentations on the economy and investment strategy. Some committees even debate the wisdom of holding particular stocks. Of course, these discussions are quite stimulating and may be necessary to maintain the interest of committee members, but it is critical for investment committees to ensure that they devote the necessary time and resources to policy decisions. Although consultants can provide useful information and guidance, trustees who are legally responsible ultimately must make policy decisions.

Developing a Manager Structure

Once the investment committee agrees on a target asset allocation, the next step is to hire investment managers in each category. The most straightforward approach is to invest in index funds, which are designed to passively track the performance of a given market. By following this approach, an institution can be assured of marketlike performance within the portion of the fund for which index funds are available or most categories of stocks, bonds, and real estate investment trusts (REITS). An added benefit is that index funds provide a level of diversification that makes it unnecessary to employ multiple managers. In other words, the marketable portion of the fund could prudently be managed by a single index fund provider, which could result in important administrative efficiencies.

However, most committees are not content to accept market returns despite the evidence, which suggests that index funds typically outperform approximately two-thirds of active managers. An institution that chooses active management typically selects a number of investment advisors with different styles to ensure that returns do not deviate too much from market indices or peer universes. To rationally select and monitor a number of managers, it is useful to develop a manager framework or structure in which each firm is selected to fill a specific role.

Two basic structures are widely used. First, the *complementary* structure calls for selecting managers with different but complementary styles. For example, an institution might select two large capitalization stock managers, one that follows a growth philosophy and a second that adheres to the value approach. The same process could be followed for the medium-sized and small capitalization segments of the market, resulting in a total of six domestic stock managers. In the bond component of the fund, the committee might choose two managers, one that anticipates changes in interest rates and a second that rotates among market sectors.

The second common framework is called the *core-satellite* approach. In this case, a low-cost, diversified core portfolio is surrounded by a number of highly focused, concentrated managers who are expected to add significant value, albeit with quite a bit of volatility. The core portfolio could be either actively or passively managed as long as it met the criteria of diversification and low cost. As was the case with "alternative assets," institutions with modest investment offices may choose to use commingled funds in order to make this process manageable.

Performance Measurement

On the one hand, trustees clearly have a fiduciary duty to monitor the performance of the endowment fund. On the other hand, a great deal of performance measurement activity is focused on short time horizons often resulting in costly and non-productive investment decisions. While there is no simple or correct approach to evaluating performance, trustees and CFOs will be well served by adhering to the following guidelines. First, it is critical to measure the performance of active managers versus appropriate benchmarks and peer universes. A great deal of what is perceived as good or bad performance is actually the result of the cyclical dominance of investment styles rather than the existence or absence of skill. Second, a fair comparison can only be made after taking into account the cost of management. Third, it is fair to evaluate returns after an appropriate adjustment for risk. And finally, many decisions to terminate managers after periods of poor performance are ill conceived because as much as twenty years of data are required to statistically demonstrate that a manager has not added value. However, it is quite appropriate to terminate a manager as a result of personnel turnover, style drift, violation of guidelines, and other similar factors.

Conclusion

Trustees have a responsibility to institute investment policies that are likely to meet their obligation to preserve the real value of endowment support for future generations. Although the CFO's role in this process will vary from one institution to the next, a minimum responsibility is to provide the committee with essential information and to ensure that it is aware of the importance of policy decisions. Specifically, it is critical that the committee establish and periodically review consistent asset allocation and spending policies. Additionally, those charged with day-to-day responsibility for endowment management must implement an appropriate risk management program and establish a fair performance measurement process. Completion of these steps does not ensure success, but the implications of failing to address these issues are serious and potentially catastrophic.

WILLIAM T. SPITZ *is treasurer of Vanderbilt University and chairman of the board of the Common Fund.*

6

The budget and its effective use as a management tool will be highlighted in this chapter. Development of a context of overall financial measurement and the creation of a structure, within which the budget communicates institutional direction to the entire community, will be discussed.

Using the Budget as an Effective Management Tool

Ronald E. Salluzzo

The institutional operating budget is a critical management tool that is capable of energizing department heads, deans, vice presidents, and others to understand their progress against institutional goals. If this statement is not consistent with the budgetary methods and activities at your institution, then you may be missing an opportunity to focus your college or university on achieving its goals.

In many organizations, the chief financial officer (CFO) is charged with responsibility for achievement of budgetary goals. Most often the decisions on spending patterns are established in the budget and then executed by a diverse, decentralized group of institutional managers. This pattern is most true for institutions of higher education.

Generally, the context within which the budget is established initially determines how budgets and the budgetary process are viewed. To make the budget document a vibrant management tool, each institutional constituency must view the budget both as a document that helps advance the institutional mission and also as a means of measuring progress toward goals for the period covered by the budget. The phrase *covered by the budget* is significant because too often the timeframe is limited to a single year. If the budget is to demonstrate direction in a meaningful way, then CFOs should consider using budget periods that match service cycles.

Effective Collaborative Planning

Most colleges and universities have, at one time or another, developed an institutional strategic plan. Strategic planning is a substantial undertaking

New Directions for Higher Education, no. 107, Fall 1999 © Jossey-Bass Publishers

61

that consumes significant resources. As a result of the planning process, each constituent of the institution reads the final plan in relation to his or her own interests. In effect, board members, senior administrators, faculty, students, and other interested parties in the campus community will view the strategic plan as a series of steps in an action plan fulfilling specific and generally different promises to each group.

If the context of the plan (that is, the institutional mission) is unclear, the strategic plan can become a document that divides rather than unifies the institutional community around the institutional mission. This division occurs when promises in the plan are not fulfilled or when affected departments do not have communication about goal achievement.

Figure 6.1 graphically depicts a planning process lacking cohesiveness between the strategic plan and the budget. If the operating budget becomes the driving force of the institution, the institution will have difficulty creating collaborative efforts. If the strategic plan, mission, core values, and vision of the institution are not clearly articulated through the budgetary process, then it is reasonable to assume that there will be substantial disagreement within the institution regarding resource allocation.

To create collaboration, the commitments that the institution makes must tie the mission directly to the budget, with the budget representing the plan's limiting factor or affordability index. The strategic planning process is the time and place for discussion and conclusions on resource allocations. This type of collaborative effort requires a strategic planning process that is both dynamic in nature and revisited each year. The appropriate starting point for decisions related to programmatic priorities is within the strategic plan, updated each year for changing and emerging circumstances.

Properly executed, the budget represents the implementation of the strategic plan over a shorter time horizon. Should planned strategies prove unaffordable, then the budgetary process should be structured to identify affordability issues.

An institution that creates collaboration between planning and budgeting generally is one with clear direction (as defined through its mission and strategic plan) and focus in achieving the goals established in the strategic plan. This implies that the strategic plan is a document focused on what the institution is attempting to become and not a compilation of wish lists promising constituencies their desires. Figure 6.2 highlights a strategic planning structure that improves collaboration because communication about institutional activities comes from a central point that generally has input from a wide variety of people.

An institution should be driven by its mission that is articulated through its strategic plan and limited by its financial resources. Each of the individual unit plans within the institution are established to achieve the goals of the strategic plan. The operating budget informs each of the individual plans about affordability of activities. A structure such as this allows

**Figure 6.1. Methodology Commonly Used
to Drive the Planning Process**

the college to think in terms of the reallocation of resources to meet its mission and also allows assessment of institutional reinvestments in physical capital, human capital, and new program initiatives.

The concept that budgets demonstrate institutional investment and reinvestment in mission-critical activities is difficult to understand if the budget is by school, department, or expense classification. Although this structure may aid department heads in understanding and managing costs, there needs to be a separate presentation of information that informs the community about institutional investment activities. The size of the investments should be articulated in the strategic plan and demonstrated each year in quantifiable amounts in the budget.

Having the budget fit within the overall strategic plan of the institution ensures that each manager in the organization understands the direction that the organization is taking. Each manager should function in ways that support advancement of the mission. Within the context of budgeting, an institution must consider several key concepts for the budget to be realistic and to meet the operating needs of the institution.

Creating a Measurement System

A key component of continuing collaborative efforts is communication between the operating managers and central administration regarding financial and nonfinancial performance. For an operating manager to understand success, communication needs to be structural in nature, relatively frequent, and repeatable at any time. The institution must establish key performance indicators that make sense within the context of the budget. Too often

Figure 6.2. A Mission-Driven Model

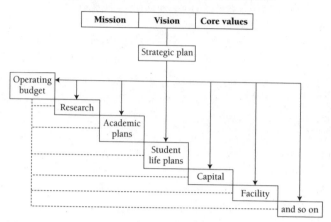

performance indicators are determined by evaluating whether the department met (or was a bit below) its expense goals. The missing piece is whether the department produced whatever units of measure that are required for the money spent. For example, if the admissions office indicates that it is under budget in its costs and yet only recruited 95 percent of the budgeted students, this would appear to be an inappropriate measure of success. For an enrollment management office to enroll all students required but at a higher-than-affordable discount rate would also be an inappropriate measure of success.

These two examples are relatively simple and straightforward and can be measured in almost every institution. However, measures of success are required for each department that has budgetary authority. The key measures need to be developed collaboratively and accepted by the department if they are to be effective.

Outcomes measures should be agreed to as part of the development of the strategic plan and should be monitored at critical junctures to understand whether or not the plan is successful, both in totality and in individual components. The measurements that an institution might use should include at least the following topics: (1) the institution as a learning organization; (2) institutional infrastructure; (3) student, faculty, and administration satisfaction; and (4) financial metrics. It is critical that only a few measures be used to identify institutional success, just as few measures should be used to measure performance at the department level.

Financial measures that an institution would use represent limiting factors, not drivers. For example, if a strategic plan puts demands on the resources of the institution that would put the institution in a clearly unhealthy financial position, then the affordability of the planned activity should be challenged. Conversely, if the anticipated financial position of the institution is strong as a result of the implementation of the strategic plan, but the key performance indicators are poor, then it would appear reasonable to assume that the institution was on a track for failure.

Each institution must select its own unique measures of success and create some level of consensus that those measures are in fact valid for the institution. From a financial perspective, these measures should include a blend of ending financial position at each measurement point and operating performance for those same periods. (This chapter does not address nonfinancial measures that usually are developed by other departments.)

Creating Overall Success Factors. A key question that senior managers and boards should ask is whether the institution's strategies are affordable. A few financial indicators can help an institution determine the answer.

The affordability of the strategic plan may be assessed by use of a select and limited number of financial ratios that can be blended to understand the financial performance of the institution. KPMG, LLP, and Prager McCarthy & Sealy developed the ratios that are in relatively common use today, and "Measuring Past Performance to Chart Future Direction" describes them in detail. An institution may wish to consider selecting the following four ratios to become overall institutional measures:

- *The viability ratio* is calculated by dividing expendable net assets by long-term. Expendable net assets are equal to the sum of unrestricted net assets; temporarily restricted net assets, and property, plant, and equipment less plant debt (including all notes, bonds, and losses to finance those fixed assets).
- *The return on net assets ratio* is calculated by dividing the change in net assets by total net assets.
- *The primary reserve ratio* is calculated by dividing expendable net assets by total expenses.
- *The net income ratio* is calculated by dividing the change in unrestricted net assets by total unrestricted income.

These four ratios were selected because they consistently measure key components of an institution in relation to an institutional risk. For example, outstanding debt by itself is not a particularly informative number. But within the context of institutional usable retained wealth, relative debt levels provide a basic understanding of the institution's capital structure and the affordability of its debt. Expendable net assets provide insight into whether the institution's financial operating size is reasonable within the context of wealth. The return that the institution has been able to achieve, both in terms of current operating size and in terms of total wealth, are key indicators of overall financial performance.

Creating a Structure to Communicate Strategy Implementation

How does an institution begin the process of aligning all of its operating plans (budgets) to its strategies? Because each institution is unique—both in its vision and its current challenges—it is difficult to prescribe a defined set of steps to follow. However, each institution should implement certain activities and decisions that will create a structure allowing planning and budgeting to be articulated and to communicate a consistent message to the institutional community.

The starting point is the creation of clearly stated goals in the strategic plan. Each initiative that the institution is addressing should specify its goals, resources (financial, capital, human, and informational) allocated or reallocated, required new revenues and their sources (if any), and key success indicators. Without clearly defined goals, resources, and performance measures, it is highly likely that the initiative will not receive adequate support and consequently will not be implemented.

The university must determine its key success indicators in the strategic plan. Key success indicators should be established for *each* key initiative and should include both nonfinancial indicators (as the drivers) and financial indicators (to create an affordability measure). The indicators should be few readily communicated to the campus community.

Once the strategic plan clearly defines institutional initiatives, the framework for creation of other plans is established. The college should require each unit preparing plans to use the same framework to ensure consistency in the development of its operating plans, both financial and nonfinancial. For some institutions, more comprehensive measures will be needed, but these will probably measure success within the organization, with fewer institutional measures. The focus always should be to measure the few items that allow determination of a plan's success. Because no activities in an institution that nonessential to its mission (or they would have been eliminated), each activity should have its own measurement.

Most institutions appear to create dynamic strategies to move the institution forward. However, if institutional plans require substantial leaps and the detail plans, both financial and nonfinancial, are incremental, the institution will likely not meet its strategic goals. Resultant plans may be balanced from an accounting perspective but not from a strategic perspective. Resources required to strategically balance institutional plans do not go away, but must be invested in a future year. This results in backloading the strategic plan. Some organizations that find a need to modify their goals in the last year of a strategic plan actually created the shortfall in its early years. Figure 6.3 illustrates this point.

When developing plans, always begin with the initiatives in the strategic plan, *not* the prior year's results. There are two relatively simple but critical elements for operating plans or budgets to articulate to the strategic plan. *Always* provide budget amounts for the initiatives first, not as an add-

Figure 6.3. Balanced Planning

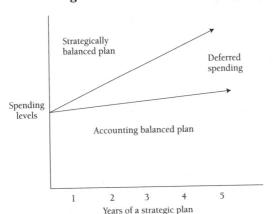

on, or the initiative will get lost. Second, always keep the amount for strategic initiatives as a separate component of the overall budget.

If the starting point is the prior year's budget, then the plan will be incremental: the size of the increment will be defined by overall institutional growth. This will ensure that funding for key initiatives is placed in the budget before resource limitations affect the budget. This is not to say that some of these allocations won't be removed later, but if they are, the amount and impact on the initiative can be defined.

Each department affected by the strategic initiatives will be required to change existing activities. If the initiative is viewed simply as another task to be performed, it may not receive high enough priority to ensure achievement. The department must translate the initiative to specific action steps and determine the resources needed—or the monetary impact of the initiative on the department.

Each department affected by the strategic initiatives must begin its planning process by defining its required activities to achieve the initiative, and then "monitize" the activity, that is, determine the necessary resources. The college next identifies the sources of revenue that will fund institutional initiatives and growth in the operating budget. Some institutions prefer to begin their budgeting process with anticipated revenue sources. In the short run, this ensures budgets balanced from an accounting perspective. Care must be taken in this process to ensure that creative ideas have an opportunity to surface and become funded.

A Sample Budgetary Process

The following simplified example illustrates how one department might respond to its responsibility in implementing a particular initiative. Assume that an institution has four strategic initiatives identified:

1. Increase student population.
2. Change the arts curriculum to improve use of technology.
3. Reassess intercollegiate athletics league affiliation.
4. Establish a stronger student satisfaction program.

The defined strategic initiative is to increase the overall on-campus student population over five years.

This example also assumes that structures such as faculty offices, dining halls, classrooms, and student facilities are adequate for the increased population. Stated differently, the institution will use unfilled capacity with this initiative.

Attainment of this goal will require the on-campus student population to grow by the numbers shown in Tables 6.1 and 6.2. Note that the initiative has three defined key success factors that are not financial: (1) the number of students enrolled per year, (2) the retention rate each year (this would be calculated from the freshman, sophomore, and junior cohorts using the prior year enrolled and current year enrolled), and (3) the graduation rate. This is a secondary measure because there is no reason to believe the added student population would have a different graduation rate than the general institutional population. The established retention rate would likely provide key input on whether the institution was meeting the needs of a larger population of students. The number enrolled is, of course, the first measure of

Table 6.1. Target On-Campus Population Increase

	Total Population	Cumulative Change (%)
Currently	8,000	
Year 1	8,480	8
Year 2	8,640	9
Year 3	8,720	10
Year 4	8,800	11
Year 5	8,880	12

Table 6.2. Determining Key Success Indicators

Year	Expected Maturation	Retention Rate (%)	Graduation Rate (%)
1	8,480	73	75
2	8,640	75	75
3	8,720	77	75
4	8,800	80	75
5	8,880	85	75

whether the initiative is succeeding. Depending on institutional circumstances, other measures such as net tuition per student may be a key success indicator. A good strategy for the institution may be to focus measures on whether the incremental students cause overcrowding that adversely effects success rates for students.

Note that market studies, a business plan, and specific operating plans typically would support the previous example. For illustrative purposes, these have been excluded.

After determining the key success factors, this institution has established the framework for translating the strategic plan into operation. The budgetary process has begun with the identification of strategic initiatives; the next step is to "monitize" or price the required activities to meet the strategic initiatives. Table 6.3 presents the monitization of the first initiative.

For example, to achieve the increase in student enrollment, central administration may decide that it needs to recruit students from geographic areas unfamiliar to the institution. This may require an investment in personnel, such as admission officers, or at least a reallocation of efforts by existing officers. The first set of activities in the enrollment management plan would be to address this initiative, and the first entry in the budget would be the required resource support.

A typical departmental budget sheet using this approach may look like Table 6.4. (Note that the document would be completed from left to right.)

Table 6.5 matches expected revenue sources with the costs identified in the budget. Note that each revenue source is identified with the related initiative and that the amounts of reallocated resources are identified in the process.

Table 6.3. Operating Budget Resources Necessary for This Initiative

Year	Admissions Staff ($)	Marketing Materials ($)	Other Operating Costs ($)	Annual Total Increase ($)
1	200	100	300	600
2	210	100	190	500
3	220	50	130	400
4	230	50	70	350
5	250	50	50	350

Note: Table 6.3 presents the institution's estimate of the incremental resources required in each of the years included in the strategic plan. The required resources are presented by major natural categories. The separation by major natural category is important so an institution can understand the portions of the intiative that represent one time investments and the portions that represent continuing investments.

Amounts shown represent thousands of dollars.

Table 6.4. Admission Department: Year 1 Operating Budget

	Support for Institutional Initiatives				Core Budget ($)	Total ($)	Per Year Budget ($)
	1	2	3	4			
Salaries and benefits	$200				3,500	3,700	3,570
Travel and conferences	$300				500	800	510
Telephone and marketing	$100				1,000	1,000	1,100
Total operating budget for the department	$600				5,000	5,600	5,100
Amounts reallocated in current year from the core budget to institutional initiatives							100

Note: Amounts have been grouped to simplify the example. Because the admissions office has no activities associated with initiatives 2, 3, and 4, these have been left blank.
   Amounts shown represent thousands of dollars.

Table 6.5. Identifying the Sources of Funds

	Initiative 1	Initiative 2	Initiative 3	Initiative 4	Core Activities	Summary of Total Budget
New resources generated by the initiative	1,600					1,600
New resources from core activities: tuition net					120,000	120,000
Investment					40,000	40,000
Composite of other sources		3,000	3,000	3,000	52,400	61,400
Reallocation of resources	100	2,000	2,000	1,900	<6,000>	
Total resources	1,700	5,000	5,000	4,900	206,400	223,000
Summary of fund usage (from detail budget sheets)	600	10,000	8,000	5,000	196,400	220,000
Net budgeting for year 1	1,100	<5,000>	<3,000>	<100>	9,800	3,000

Note: Amounts shown represent thousands of dollars.

An operating budget represents the anticipated economic wants of the institution expressed in dollars. Monitization of strategic initiatives can provide insight into the degree to which the institution has funded its strategic initiatives. By putting these together, key stakeholders should be able to establish useable expectations about institutional achievement of goals. The saying that "what gets measured gets done" seems appropriate for colleges and universities. A systemic method of measurement may well provide common ground for organizations to understand progress in organizational direction.

RONALD E. SALLUZZO is national industry director of higher education with KPMG LLP.

This chapter introduces the concept of campus master planning, describes master planning process drivers, discusses the relationship to capital budgeting, and offers a typical master planning and capital budgeting process.

Campus Master Planning and Capital Budgeting

J. Kent Caruthers, Daniel T. Layzell

Chief financial officers (CFOs) of colleges and universities spend a significant portion of their time each day focusing on their institutions' current and future financial pictures. An activity that has significant implications for both the current and future financial picture of any such institution is the development of the campus physical master plan and the determination of related capital budget needs. As a result, it is in the best interest of the CFO and the institution for the CFO to be actively involved in the master planning and capital budgeting processes.

We should note at the outset that there are various perspectives on campus master planning and capital budgeting ranging from a narrow focus to a broader, more comprehensive vision. Our particular perspective is more the latter, stressing the interrelationships among academic planning, strategic planning, physical planning, and resource requirements planning. Although the most visible results of campus master planning and capital budgeting are often physical changes to the campus landscape, we believe that form must follow function. That is, each of these activities, including campus master planning and capital budgeting, must be an integrated part of the overall vision and planning horizon for an institution.

Overview of Campus Master Planning

The campus master plan is, at its essence, a statement of how the institution plans to change physically over a given period of time. It reflects the institution's mission and academic plan and, for public colleges or universities, sometimes the state's plan for higher education; it also sets the context for the future of the institution through an analysis of demographic, economic, and geographic trends impacting the campus. Another way of viewing the campus master plan is as a reality check that sets parameters for the institution's physical growth. Campus master plans outline building design and location, campus traffic patterns, utilities needs (that is, electricity, natural gas, water, and sewer), and needed land improvements or acquisitions.

Campus master plans are based on assumptions about basic campus characteristics drawn from projections of academic plans. At a minimum, these plans should include all underlying assumptions (demographic, economic, and programmatic), existing and preferred institutional building and land uses, buildings, landscape, and open space features, and pedestrian and vehicular circulation systems. Like most planning documents, campus master plans should be regularly updated as existing data and assumptions become obsolete. The planning horizon for the master plan should be at least ten years (Kaiser and Klein, 1992).

It should come as no surprise that there is a very close relationship between an institution's master plan and its capital budget. The capital budget is essentially a financial translation of the master plan. As such, the capital budget has a number of purposes: to facilitate the implementation of the master plan, to permit the exploration of financial alternatives, to help manage balance sheets, and to communicate these options to the governing board. Given that the financial requirements of a master plan may vary substantially from year to year, the objective of the capital budget should be to integrate these uneven needs smoothly into the institution's resource allocation program. Capital projects that are not adequately planned can put enormous financial strains on any institution (Dickmeyer, 1992).

Campus Master Plan Process Drivers

As discussed at the beginning of this chapter, we view campus master planning as being integrated within the overall planning framework of the institution. The campus master plan should be a logical outgrowth of the institution's overall strategic plan, which is ultimately driven by the mission of the institution. Such linkages form parameters within which the campus master plan is developed.

Projected Enrollment and Staffing Levels. Clearly, an institution's current and future enrollment levels have a significant impact on space needs. Instructional space needs in particular are directly related to enrollment. For example, if an institution is expecting enrollment to remain stable for the foreseeable future and the current level of instructional space is determined to be adequate, the CFO need not be very concerned with the construction of additional classroom space and may want to focus instead on other needs. On the other hand, if an institution is in a significant growth mode, the focus will likely be on the development of additional instructional space.

Likewise, current and future staffing levels will have an impact on institutional space needs. In particular, office space needs will be impacted by future staffing assumptions. Although minor changes in staffing levels can usually be accommodated within existing space, more significant changes can create logistical and staff morale problems if not adequately planned.

Current and Future Academic Programs. An institution's program mix has an impact on the types of instructional space needed. Likewise, anticipated changes in academic programs will have an impact on space planning for the future. For example, if an institution anticipates that there will be an increased emphasis on doctoral-level training in the sciences in the future, research laboratory space will need to be enhanced or expanded. Likewise, if an institution is phasing out particular programs, current space utilized by these programs will be freed up for other use.

Related to this are the special technology needs of distance learning. As institutions move more aggressively into this mode of instruction, new space standards must be developed for distance learning sites, both on and off campus. Further, institutions are finding it necessary to upgrade their telecommunications infrastructure to meet the demands of both synchronous (videoconferencing) and asynchronous (Web-based) distance learning.

Support Programs and Other University Activities. Related to an institution's academic program are the other programs and activities engaged in as part of the specific campus mission. Such activities include faculty research, public service and outreach (for example, cooperative extension and continuing education), intercollegiate athletics, and student organizations. Each of these areas has facilities and space needs that should be considered as part of the campus master planning process.

Current Space Use and Condition. The way an institution currently utilizes its space has a tremendous impact on future space planning. Most institutions can find ways in which to use existing space more efficiently, which then reduces the need for new construction in the future. The condition of current facilities likewise is a driver in campus master planning. An institution may determine that it is not cost efficient to renovate an existing building, thereby creating the potential need for a new building. As will be discussed later on in this chapter, the assessment of current space use and facilities condition are two of the initial activities in any campus master planning process.

Land Availability. The ability of an institution to grow physically is obviously affected by the availability of land on which to place new facilities or other improvements. The location of an institution usually plays a major role in determining land availability. For example, urban institutions typically face greater constraints in acquiring additional acreage than do institutions in more rural settings, although this is not always the case. A related factor is the extent to which any new land acquired would need to be developed (such as putting in utilities and roads) before it could be used, which is often an issue for more rural institutions.

Health, Safety, and Accessibility Issues. Another set of factors to be considered in the master planning process are health, safety, and accessibility issues. Many times, the way in which an institution responds to such issues will be proscribed by federal, state, and local regulatory requirements including the Americans with Disabilities Act (ADA), the Occupational Health and Safety Act (OSHA), various environmental regulations, and state and local building codes. The implications of these laws and regulations should be kept in mind as the institution considers alternatives for future development.

Safety issues related to campus crime are increasingly important to master planning. Of particular note are concerns regarding exterior lighting, parking, emergency phones, and building security. Interestingly, campus landscaping can also play a role in facilitating or hindering criminal activity on campus.

Local Community Considerations. Given that most institutions are not islands unto themselves but instead are part of a larger community, a primary political consideration in campus master planning is the impact that the plan might have on the host town or city. For example, although a campus building renovation usually does not draw much ire from local residents, the decision to block off a city street going through the middle of campus to create a greenspace will often create tensions. Another issue that often raises tensions between the campus and community is the presence of student housing in local residential areas. As a result, some campuses have found it useful to have community leaders participate in the master planning process to ensure the chance for community input.

Architectural and Aesthetic Considerations. Institutions are increasingly concerned with the creation of a unified architectural theme for the campus because attractive buildings and grounds are often major draws for potential new students. Thus, the master plan should recognize any current theme in place. Conversely, an institution may choose to use the master plan as a chance to give the campus an architectural facelift.

Financial Considerations. Last but certainly not least in the factors to be considered in the planning process are the financial resources available to implement the master plan. Resource availability is a specific concern in capital budget development, but it is also important to be realistic in the development of the master plan. Campus staff involved in developing the master plan often get caught up in the excitement of planning for the future and as a result may propose options that exceed the institution's financial resources. Although campus master planning is a creative exercise that should push the envelope, unrealistic expectations can quickly doom a plan.

Capital Budgeting

Capital budgeting is a discipline for examining plans and alternatives for projects that could bring major changes to an institution's asset or expense structure (Dickmeyer, 1992). Capital projects usually require several years of planning and significant infusions of funding over a multiyear period.

Types of Capital Projects. Capital expenditures are typically defined as those for items that exceed a certain dollar amount threshold or have an expected life of longer than a single fiscal year. Construction of a new building is the most common example of a capital project. Other examples include renovations of existing buildings, major equipment purchases (for example, mainframe computers), infrastructure improvements, and land acquisitions.

Revenue Sources for the Capital Budget. Revenue to fund capital expenditures can come from a variety of sources. Although some institutions are fortunate enough to generate operating surpluses of sufficient magnitude to fund capital investment, more often separate funding sources are sought.

State-supported institutions typically participate in a separate process for capital budgeting than that used for operations. In some states, the legislature has designated certain revenue sources to be dedicated for capital purposes and reviews capital budget requests from institutions each year in light of projected availability of funds and competing needs. Other states attempt to fund capital programs with unbudgeted surpluses when revenue collections exceed earlier estimates.

At the institutional level, additional sources of capital funds include debt and private giving. In public colleges and universities, long-term debt is a common technique for funding facilities that house auxiliary enterprise activities (such as residence halls or bookstores) where a portion of the projected revenue stream from operations can be dedicated to repayment of the debt. In private universities and for academic buildings at public universities, a portion of the revenue stream from tuition and fees is dedicated to repayment of debt service. Capital campaigns to raise private gifts to expand or enhance facilities are also a common way to fund the capital budget.

Projection of Revenue and Expenditures. Similar to the responsibility for the operating budget, the CFO should be responsible for developing and maintaining current projections of revenue and expenditures for the capital budget. Some capital revenue streams are relatively easy to project, such as student fees for capital improvement or multiyear capital appropriations, whereas others are more problematic. Fiscal conservatism is a desired trait in projecting the results of capital campaigns.

Because capital projects often take several years to complete, the projection of expenditures needs to be detailed by period. Not only inflation but also terms for payments to contractors based on progress in completing the project must be taken into consideration.

Impact of Capital Budget on Operating Budget. Another financial planning consideration in managing the capital budget is its impact on the operating budget. Obvious examples include the need to increase the budget for custodial services, utilities, and maintenance reserves for new facilities. Sometimes, however, a capital expenditure can contribute to a reduction in operating costs, such as when new structures permit the demolition of older buildings that are more costly to maintain or the cancellation of leases for temporary space.

Just as capital budget decisions can have impact on the operating budget, the reverse is also true. For instance, the failure to provide adequate funding for routine building maintenance in the operating budget will eventually lead to a requirement for a capital budget item for deferred maintenance. Likewise, a decision to purchase rather than lease major equipment can shift expenditure requirements between the capital and operating budgets.

Typical Master Planning and Capital Budgeting Processes

The successful approaches used by colleges and universities to develop their master plans and prepare their capital budgets share a number of common traits.

Establish Steering Committee and Communications Plan. Most colleges and universities create a broadly based committee to oversee the master planning process. The typical committee will include representatives from the faculty, academic administration, student services, business and finance, the student body, alumni, and the local community. A planning committee with this diversity serves to ensure that many different points of view are heard and inform planning decisions. A planning committee also contributes to greater acceptance of recommendations. As such, an initial activity by the steering committee should be the development and adoption of guiding principles and priorities to assist in the planning process.

A second consideration in the establishment of a steering committee is the need for staff support. Although some schools expect the committee members to undertake their own special studies, many colleges have found it more desirable to assign professional staff to assist the committee in its work. Staff members typically are drawn from the institutional research and planning office, the facilities planning office, and the budget office.

Depending on the complexity of the issues to be addressed and the availability of staff to be assigned to support the committee, an institution may find it necessary and beneficial to retain an external consultant. A common arrangement is to hire a consulting team that includes both educational planners and architects. In this situation, the educational planners review enrollment projections, assess the need for potential new programs, and forecast future staffing levels, while the architects consider issues related to physical site location and campus circulation patterns.

An important consideration in the work of the steering committee is to maintain an effective program of communications with the campus community. Members of the committee can play a key role in this regard by reporting back to their respective constituencies. Other methods for maintaining communications that have proven effective are town hall meetings and periodic newsletters.

Conduct an Environmental Scan. One of the key analytic approaches used in strategic master planning is the environmental scan, the purpose of which is to identify and then to understand the trends that are shaping the institution, and especially its need for facilities. Environmental scans should consider both the internal and external forces affecting the institution.

The scan of the internal environment should take into account how the institution's unique history and traditions and the evolution of its programs, personnel, and operating styles will affect the types of facilities needed in the future. Although the master plan generally is a device to document how program changes might affect land use and facilities, the history and tradition of an institution can also influence the master plan. For example, most campuses have visual landmarks (perhaps a bell tower) that have become part of the identity of the institution. Similarly, campuses often have outdoor gathering areas, such as a quad that alumni recall with fondness. In developing a master plan, such features are often reemphasized or even replicated on other parts of the campus to provide a sense of continuity.

The scan of the external environment should include analyses of changing demographic, social, and economic circumstances. For instance, a baby boom may indicate likely enrollment growth with the requirement for additional space. Concerns about personal safety may dictate changes in new building design and open space configuration. Economic-related considerations include energy prices, student parking and transportation requirements, and the movement toward outsourcing.

Set Goals and Establish Priorities. A common result of preliminary master planning efforts is a set of potential actions that either are in conflict with one another or greatly exceed the resources of the institution to implement. When this occurs, attention needs to shift to some type of goal- or priority-setting activity. As noted at the beginning of this section, the master planning process will ideally have begun with the establishment by the steering committee of a set of guiding principles and priorities to assist in this exercise.

Assess Current/Future Space Needs. Except in the special set of circumstances where a totally new campus is being planned, a major part of the master planning effort must be the analysis of existing space. A comprehensive analysis of existing space includes

- an inventory of what now exists
- an assessment of the physical condition by type and amount of space
- an assessment of the suitability of the space for the programs offered
- determination of any special conditions or features such as the ability to accommodate technology or the degree of accessibility

- an identification of the extent that the space is used for its various purposes
- a calculation of the capacity of the space

For public institutions, approximately one-half of the states have adopted space analysis standards and models for the state-level capital budgeting process that also can be used in the assessment of the adequacy of existing space for the institutional master plan. These models typically relate the numbers of students to be served by major and level to space needs based on various space use standards and allowances per student or staff member.

Establish Master Planning Alternatives and Cost Estimates. Generally the master planning process will lead to a limited number of alternative scenarios to be considered. Each of the scenarios should satisfy the major goals and objectives but may differ in their degree of accomplishment of lesser objectives and their impact on existing programs.

When the master plan calls for new construction, decisions must be made not only about which program(s) will occupy the new space but also about how the space being vacated will be reassigned among other units. This domino effect often ripples through five or six departments before each unit is settled in its newly assigned space. The extent of disruption on existing programs is a key consideration in choosing among alternative scenarios.

Typically, the most important factor in choosing among alternative scenarios is cost. Detailed cost estimates need to be prepared that outline both the capital cost (for example, site preparation, infrastructure, construction, and fixed equipment) and the operating cost (for example, relocation expense, temporary facilities, and ongoing maintenance).

Identify Revenue Sources. As noted earlier, the capital budgeting process involves the identification of available sources of revenue to fund the implementation of the master plan. Once the major decisions in the planning process approach conclusion, a more specific linking of funding to projects is needed. The sequence and phasing of plan implementation is often contingent on availability of funds.

Finalize a Master Plan. One of the final steps in the master planning process is the preparation of the final report. A typical master planning report will provide the following:

- Background information about the institution
- A discussion of the results of the environmental scan
- A presentation of the academic plan
- A summary of the findings of the assessment of existing facilities
- The recommended scenario
- The funding strategy
- A time line and phasing schedule

The planning report should include both overview and detail site maps that show both the existing and planned conditions and architectural renderings of any significant design elements that serve to define the plan.

Implement and Monitor. Perhaps the greatest challenge for an institution in carrying out a master planning activity is not to produce a plan that sits on the shelf when completed rather than serving as a guide for campus development. An effective way to make sure that the plan is effective is to establish an implementation and monitoring process.

Because published master plans tend to be written in global terms, a more detailed version is often needed for internal management. The more detailed version should include specific schedules and deadlines for accomplishing each component of the plan. With such information, the CFO (who often holds ultimate responsibility for implementation of the physical aspects of the plan) can assign specific responsibility to staff members and contractors for elements of the plan and then monitor their progress toward achievement of the plan.

Conclusion

Developing a comprehensive institutional master plan can have profound impacts on the future success and viability of the institution. A well-conceived and well-executed master planning and capital budgeting process can help to focus scarce institutional resources on developing quality programs that meet the needs of campus constituents. Conversely, poorly designed processes can lead to significant financial and political problems for an institution.

References

Dickmeyer, N. "Budgeting." In D. Greene (ed.), *College and University Business Administration.* Washington, D.C.: NACUBO, 1992.
Kaiser, H., and Klein, E. "Facilities Management." In D. Greene (ed.), *College and University Business Administration.* Washington, D.C.: NACUBO, 1992.

J. KENT CARUTHERS *is senior partner and deputy CEO of MGT of America, Inc., in Tallahassee, Florida.*

DANIEL T. LAYZELL *is a principal of MGT of America, Inc., in Tallahassee, Florida.*

8

The buildings, people, and mission of an institution are inevitably exposed to risks that must be concerns of the CFO. This chapter describes physical, casualty, fiscal, business, and reputational risk, and provides examples of effective risk management.

Identifying and Managing Risk

Janice M. Abraham

Risk management is not the elimination of risk; rather it is dealing with risk in the most effective and sensible manner while supporting the mission of our institutions and the inherent risk our students, faculty, staff, and volunteers encounter in pursuit of teaching, research, and student activities. When developing a risk management program, it would be easy to forget that colleges and universities exist so that students and faculty can take risks; experimentation, testing new ideas, and trying new activities are part of the education experience.

The role of a chief financial officer (CFO) on campus, whether addressing risk management, overseeing capital projects, or building a budget, is a holistic one, weaving together a cross section of the campus community and balancing conflicting priorities. It is the business officers' role to see the total cost (that is, both hard and soft costs) of any initiative on campus, and risk management is no exception. *Hard costs* are the actual dollars expended to correct the problem, the tangible or objective cost of the loss. The *soft costs*, while not easily quantifiable, are also very real. They include the emotional damage to the community, the grief and distraction a loss causes and the reputational loss of the institution's good name. Understanding the components and total cost of a successful risk management program and supplying the building blocks for the program are the goals of this chapter.

The specific role of the chief financial officer is to

- Identify risk
- Develop a campus plan to reduce and control risk
- Transfer risk
- Track and report the cost of risk management

Identification and Reduction of Risk

The types of risk are as varied and complex as each campus. Most risks, however, fall within the following five categories: physical, casualty, fiscal, business, and reputational.

Physical Risk. Buildings, both new and historic; laboratories; art collections; remote research stations; vehicles; and a myriad of other items are significant institutional assets. The cost of replacing them if they are damaged and the loss of income if normal events can not transpire are the hard costs of physical risks. In addition, the disruption to the community if a major building (a library, residence hall, or science lab) is destroyed is incalculable. The scale of the damage is exponential if the building has special historic value.

Physical risk takes many forms and strikes in various ways. Fire; earthquakes; weather-related events including ice, windstorms, and floods; and vandalism are the most common and devastating culprits. Also of concern are damage to buildings and land by pollutants from leaking tanks, accidental spills, or careless disposal procedures.

Casualty Risk. Casualty risk is the risk that someone will accuse the institution of doing something wrong either by its actions or management decisions. It takes many forms, from negligence on the part of administrators to a tragic accident. These risks are grouped into two broad categories: general liability to others for physical injury or damage to that party's property and legal liability arising from management decisions, for example, employment decisions such as wrongful termination, gender or age discrimination, or suits against the governing board on its decisions on the operations of the institutions. Auto liability and workers' compensation are also casualty risks.

Fiscal Risk. The financial assets of the campus—endowments, trusts and deferred gifts, working capital, and federal and state funds—often rival the monetary value of the physical assets. Fiscal risks also take many forms: investment risk and asset allocation decisions of the endowment funds, poor operating procedures with federal or outside funds, or employee theft and dishonesty.

Business Risk. The business of a college or university is teaching, research, and service. Potential events that can disrupt or damage these goals are business risks. An economic downturn in the region may threaten a successful enrollment plan with the right mix of students and the budgeted amount of financial aid; another research university may sign an agreement for a new technology that supplants a major new initiative from the university's lab; a for-profit entity may offer a program that competes with the profitable continuing education program; or a popular and successful president may move to another institution halfway through a capital campaign.

Reputational Risk. The ivory tower, which protected and preserved the institutions in the past, is under siege by the press, legislators, business, and even students, our customers. Failure to achieve good risk management in any of the categories mentioned here places the reputation of the institution at risk.

Physical Risk and Workplace Safety. A comprehensive facilities program is the best place to identify physical risks and the associated risk of workplace hazards. Identifying and eliminating deferred maintenance, incorporating life safety reviews in minor and major maintenance, an ongoing maintenance program, and thorough review of all major renovations and new construction projects will facilitate early identification of risks.

A team is necessary to identify physical risk:

- Users of the facilities are the first lines of defense in identifying risks in facilities. A maintenance work order system that is user friendly will encourage students, staff, and faculty to report problems early. Overloaded circuits, broken stairs, and poor lighting are accidents waiting to happen and can be identified and corrected before problems arise. Creating a feedback system that encourages faculty and staff to comment on workplace issues serves the dual purpose of helping to identify problems and letting the community know that the institution values workplace safety.
- Maintenance and custodial staff are integral to identifying risks. Training them to identify problems in facilities and report their observations in a regular manner is a powerful tool.
- Outside experts, architects, engineers, and insurance company loss-control specialists fulfill needed technical review of projects.

Legal Liability. Liability risks occur when events don't happen as planned. Problems happen when policies and procedures establishing the appropriate and desired outcome don't exist, are poorly written or are not followed.

Employment Practices. Compensation accounts for half of an institution's budget; accordingly, the potential for significant risk resulting from employment actions is a major concern owing to the nature of lifelong employment through tenure and the close-knit nature of campus communities. Additional problems arise from the lack of coordination among academic personnel offices and other personnel offices. On most campuses, responsibilities for personnel policies are divided between the human resource or personnel office and the academic affairs office, which is responsible for the hiring, promotion, and tenure of faculty.

Policies, procedures, training, and an audit on the effectiveness of the following policies are the first steps in identifying and reducing risks in employment practices:

- Sexual harassment (including faculty, staff, and students)
- Hiring

Testing and background checks for staff
Clear explanations of expectations for faculty
- Performance and compensation reviews
- Professional development and ongoing training
- Discipline and termination

Training is most effective when it has the clear support of senior administration and reaches those on the front line of decision making. Academic department chairs, supervisors in administrative departments, and leaders in the maintenance departments are examples of employees that need regular training.

Outside assistance from legal counsel with expertise in employment practices is essential. The laws governing employment practices are complex and evolving. Expert advice on the development of policies, creation of training programs, and auditing effectiveness is critical. For example, prior to termination of an employee, an independent review of the institution's adherence to its own policies of performance review, discipline, and termination can mitigate or eliminate later problems.

General Liability. Policies, procedures, and training are themes that resonate throughout liability risk management. In the general liability area, these take on added importance because the risks are not only purely monetary but also include personal injury. Campuses often are considered public spaces and are perceived to be without borders. This openness, although a vital part of the learning environment, increases the risk that people will be hurt. An effective risk management program follows the activities on campus to identify and reduce liability risk. Significant areas of concern include

- Vehicle safety programs including van driver training for student groups, and athletic teams as well as training for faculty leading field trips
- Substance abuse training, binge drinking, and sexual misconduct associated with substance abuse
- Foreign study safety, including travel safety and emergency evacuation plans
- Fitness and athletic facilities including staffing and correct use of equipment
- Premises surveillance and fire safety programs to identify hazards and correct them, including emergency response procedures
- Security issues both in buildings and on campus

Controlling Risk

Disasters are by their nature unpredictable; they can range from a sniper in the clock tower, a van accident in a remote area, a serial killer in the neighborhood, a hazardous chemical leak in the community, floods, mudslides, fires, and earthquakes. A plan should be developed with the full involvement of the entire campus, and it should be tested and reviewed annually. Changes reflecting new staff, new equipment, phone numbers, and resources should be incorporated in the plan. An experienced business officer reports that in a crisis three things must happen: students must be fed, water (potable and waste) must flow, and faculty and staff must be paid!

A school should have a plan for responding to serious accidents that occur off campus. Having a team, including a senior staff member with authorization to spend money as needed, immediately travel to the accident is important. Establishing a crisis center on campus that can call parents, coordinate the homecoming of injured students, and answer questions from the press is needed. Ongoing support from counselors and health professionals when the students, faculty, and staff return to campus allows the institution to manage problems that may arise after the resumption of normal campus life.

Transferring Risk

While an institution is identifying, reducing, and controlling risk it should also recognize that transferring or sharing some of the risk is an essential tool. Buying insurance is the primary means to transfer risk. Another method is to include appropriate insurance requirements and enforceable indemnity clauses in construction, service, and supply contracts. Establishing clear authority for signing contracts is important for oversight and control of the institution's obligations.

The history, practices, and nuances of purchasing insurance could fill many volumes. The basic points for a business officer to know include how much risk to transfer, what type of risk should be transferred, and what insurance companies best meet the institution's needs.

The question of how much risk to transfer involves both the amount of risk an institution retains and the limits of insurance that an institution buys. A self-insured retention, sometimes called a *deductible,* is the amount of money an institution pays on a claim prior to the insurance company paying. All things being equal, the lower the deductible, the more that specific type of insurance will cost. An institution with strong risk management and a good history of losses may be more willing to trade off today's dollars in lower premiums for a higher deductible knowing that if a loss occurs it will share in the costs by paying the costs within the deductible. Decision making on the level of the deductible should incorporate the price trade-off as well as the institution's financial resources and tolerance for risk.

Selecting proper limits is difficult. Legal and general liability losses can be very high, into the tens of millions of dollars. Most institutions select limits based on the practices of peers, consideration of the local conditions, and the courts' propensity to make large judgments. Given the dire consequences of large, underinsured losses, institutions should prefer to assume more under the deductible and use the savings to purchase sufficient limits.

Property Insurance. Although most institutions know that property insurance covering physical damage to buildings and their contents is essential, care must be taken to make sure the coverage is adequate. Most institutions today insure on an all-risk basis for the replacement cost of the property. All-risk insurance covers all losses except for those specifically excluded. Consider removing standard exclusions such as those covering flood, earthquake, and theft, that could lead to significant loss. Replacement cost will pay for the rebuilding the property without deduction for depreciation; it will not cover the cost of including mandated enhancements such as those required by the Americans with Disabilities Act (ADA) or building codes. Without special agreements, insurance may not cover the cost to replace special building features such as stone carvings.

Property insurance can cover the financial impact resulting from a fire or other accident and can cover the loss of tuition and fees if the campus shuts down or the extra expenses to keep it running.

Liability. All institutions should purchase general liability, educators' legal liability (including employment practice), auto liability, and an excess or umbrella policy that adds additional limits to these basic policies.

Institutions should consider their need for other liability policies as well. These include fiduciary liability, covering the proper handling of employee benefit plans and assets; environmental liability, covering clean-up and other issues resulting from pollution events; police legal liability, covering the action of security personnel; and medical malpractice, covering claims arising from care given in the infirmary.

Insuring Other Risks. Although large corporations use risk transfer for insuring business risks, this concept is not put in practice at universities. As institutions move more aggressively into entrepreneurial ventures, distance learning, technology transfer, and so on, it is likely that risk previously viewed as uninsurable will be transferred through insurance.

The Role of Others in Risk Management

Effective risk management programs include the entire community. Smaller colleges that can not financially support a risk manager should consider sharing one with neighboring colleges or participating in a group insurance and risk management program. Human resource staff can take the lead with management training programs. Colleges dependent on outside counsel should take steps to keep them current on higher education issues.

Insurance is purchased through brokers or agents who are also a valuable resource. Identify an insurance broker who views his or her role as that of a consultant rather than that of a salesperson. Changing the broker's compensation to a consulting fee rather than a percentage of the insurance premium sends a message as to his or her role as problem solver.

The senior administration and governing boards are the final link in the risk management chain, which begins with the faculty, staff, and students; moves through the risk manager and business officer; and draws on the knowledge of attorneys, brokers, and other experts. It is the CFO's role to establish a clear link to the governing board, creating a reporting relationship with the board audit committee to regularly review

- The limits of the institution's insurance, including the amount of retention or deductible for each policy
- The company providing the insurance, including its financial condition and rating (AM Best provides a rating on the financial strength of insurance companies)
- Risk management programs that are in place (including a crisis management plan) and their effectiveness, through an audit process
- Benchmarking reports of the total cost of risk management

Business officers wear many hats. The most important is that of the guardian of the institution's assets. Risk management in all it forms—identifying, reducing, controlling, and transferring risk—is an invaluable tool for safeguarding those assets.

JANICE M. ABRAHAM is president and CEO of United Educators Insurance Risk Retention Group, Inc., Chevy Chase, Maryland.

9

Interest in consortia among colleges and universities has never been higher. This chapter describes Five Colleges, Inc., one of the oldest consortia, and discusses both the advantages and challenges of collaborative relationships.

Financing Participation in Consortia

Mary Jo Maydew

As higher education becomes a more competitive industry and as controlling costs becomes a higher priority, new relationships among institutions are emerging. One form that these new relationships take is manifested in the development of formal consortia among colleges and universities. Interest in consortia has exploded in recent years as institutions come to appreciate the advantages that such collaboration offers.

The Association for Consortium Leadership reports on its Web site (www.acl.odu.edu) that there are approximately 125 consortia in the United States, varying in size from 3 to over 100 members. One of the oldest, Five Colleges, Inc.—a consortium of Amherst, Hampshire, Mount Holyoke, and Smith Colleges and The University of Massachusetts at Amherst—was formally incorporated in 1965. A description of its structure, programs, and collaborative approaches provides a useful framework for examining how consortia can be valuable to colleges and universities.

The Five Colleges

Although the Five Colleges did not formally incorporate until 1965, their history of cooperation began in the 1950s, when there were only four institutions, with the establishment of a shared Department of Astronomy and a number of collaborative academic programs. The success of these efforts helped lay the groundwork for the next, much grander collaboration—the establishment of Hampshire College, dedicated to curricular innovation and self-defined programs of study. Hampshire College began admitting students in 1970 and became the fifth member of Five Colleges, Inc.

The Five Colleges began as a consortium focused on academic cooperation and this focus predominated throughout the 1970s and into the

1980s. A second Five Colleges department, dance, was established and the number of collaborative programs and shared faculty continued to increase. Student cross-registrations rose steadily, finally requiring the development of a transportation system among the campuses. Collaboration among the libraries proceeded from permitting open borrowing among the students of the five institutions to the current shared electronic card catalog and automated circulation and acquisitions system.

The earliest form of collaboration in administrative areas was joint purchasing of furniture and equipment. This led to the establishment in the 1970s of the Massachusetts Higher Education Consortium, a joint purchasing collaborative that now includes as members most colleges and universities in the Commonwealth of Massachusetts. Other joint administrative efforts did not begin in earnest until the late 1980s when, with the assistance of the Mellon Foundation, the Five Colleges launched a series of cooperative administrative efforts. The results include shared programs in risk management, recycling, student health insurance, employee health insurance, management training, some forms of legal services and student loan servicing, and a Five College on-line course catalog.

In many ways, Five Colleges, Inc., is similar to other consortia; however, there are some differences. Unlike most consortia, Five Colleges was established primarily to further academic cooperation and to enrich the curriculum of each of its participants. For most of its history, Five Colleges has focused on doing new things in cost-effective ways rather than on avoiding or reducing costs. Only in the last decade have cost reduction and avoidance become significant efforts of the consortium. Another difference is the combination of large and small, public and private institutions. This has made the collaboration both more complex (particularly for the University of Massachusetts, which also belongs to a five-member state university system) and more rewarding.

Benefits of Collaboration

From this brief look at the collaborative efforts of the Five Colleges, some of the benefits of consortia are apparent.

Program Enrichment. Perhaps the easiest form of cooperation is joining together to share the costs of new programs or services. Program enrichment represents an opportunity for the institutions to expand their offerings, but in a cost-effective way. A recent example at the Five Colleges is the program in Film Studies. By developing a shared program the institutions were able to resist the pressure to establish a Department of Film Studies at each campus and to build on Hampshire College's strong program in film production. Students at all of the institutions have access to a Film Studies major at a considerably lower investment than would otherwise have been the case.

Another example is the Five College Training Collaborative, a team of human resources professionals from the five institutions that has developed joint programs in management and supervisory training. The shared program has made it possible for all of the institutions to have high-quality management training at an affordable cost, providing significant benefits to the institutions.

Cost Avoidance. Although program enrichment does provide a cost-effective way to add programs and services, most institutions are looking for more from consortial efforts. Cost avoidance is the next most readily achievable form of collaboration. An example of cost avoidance is the Five College's recycling program. In response to the rapidly increasing costs of waste disposal, the Five Colleges hired a joint recycling coordinator. His task was to develop recycling programs and raise awareness so that the percentage of trash recycled continued to increase at each institution. Initially, the savings in disposal costs were roughly equal to the additional costs of the position. However, as disposal costs have continued to climb, significant costs have been avoided as the base percentage of nonrecycled material continues to decline.

An example from the academic side is the decision of the colleges' Departments of Physics to rely on the University of Massachusetts to teach a number of the upper-division undergraduate electives in physics of interest to physics majors. This allows each college's Department of Physics to offer a robust major in physics without requiring the faculty numbers needed to offer all courses at all campuses to a very small number of students.

Reducing Costs. Most consortia now being started have their impetus in finding ways to reduce costs. For existing institutions with full complements of programs and services, this is a considerably more difficult form of collaboration than those previously discussed. Opportunities to reduce costs come in several forms; sharing purchased services, integrating a previously fragmented program or service, and combining operations are three of those forms.

An example of reducing costs by sharing purchased services among the four private colleges of the consortium is joint legal services for trusts and estates. Initially, all four colleges had separate relationships for trust and estate legal services. By negotiating a shared retainer with a single firm, the colleges were able to reduce their base cost for this service by 50 percent.

The Five Colleges' approach to risk management is a good example of consolidating a fragmented service. The four private colleges each had a person who devoted a fraction of his or her time to insurance and risk management issues, and in all cases the person's training was in other areas. Risk management was an add-on to these individuals' responsibilities, and as a result the function received minimal oversight. No one college would have considered it cost effective to add a full-time professional risk manager. However, by sharing a risk manager among the four institutions, the colleges have realized significant savings, have far better insurance coverage, and are developing a strong program of risk avoidance and claims management.

By far the most difficult way to achieve cost reductions, and the approach with the greatest potential impact on consortia, is to combine existing operations. Perhaps the best example of this is Claremont College's approach, where many back-office functions in the financial and administrative areas are provided centrally. This was achievable in large part because several of the colleges were founded during the same period of time and the centralized services were in place from the beginning.

However, for institutions that are fully staffed and currently provide a full complement of programs and services, combining operations presents a number of difficulties. Combining operations is more disruptive of existing staff and the inevitably different various local approaches and is less likely to offer improved services as well as lower costs than consolidating a fragmented service. Although it is possible that a combined operation will result in better service, it is also possible that an individual campus will feel less well served. Local habits likely will need to be changed to make possible a single approach to service delivery; individual idiosyncrasies are less likely to be accommodated. Thus, the pressure to reduce costs must be significant, and the institution's leadership must strongly support a cooperative solution if combining existing operations is to have a hope of being accomplished. At Five Colleges, this is the next logical step for the consortium; we have had one or two false starts but have not yet succeeded at this most difficult form of collaboration.

The Ripple Effect of Successful Collaboration. One of the most gratifying aspects of consortia is the way in which one successful program or service begins to offer other, related opportunities in a widening circle of collaborative efforts. This has been the case with the Five Colleges risk management program. The initial program was built around hiring a shared risk manager and combining insurance coverages. In the past five years, the collaborative efforts have expanded to include shared retentions, a shared student health insurance program, a combined owner-controlled insurance program for construction projects, and plans for the development of a joint health and safety task force. Each successful collaboration provides opportunities to extend the joint efforts into related areas. This organic growth of collaborative efforts, each building on the latest successful effort, can provide substantial cost savings over time and build a strong commitment to other kinds of collaboration.

Combining Talents. Focusing more good minds on the topic at hand, whatever it may be, potentiates all forms of collaboration. If, for example, there is a financial problem to be solved anywhere in the Five Colleges, there are five chief financial officers (CFOs) available to think about the problem, and they are experienced at thinking together. Whether a collaborative solution emerges or not, the result is likely to be better because it benefits from the thinking of the whole group.

The Challenges of Collaboration

Although consortia offer many advantages for colleges and universities, collaborative efforts also have a number of challenges associated with them.

The Slow Pace of Change. Institutions of higher education are notorious for the amounts of time required to accomplish change. This is due in part to the aversion to risk that has been characteristic of much of higher education. However, it also results from the powerful process orientation that is a legacy of shared governance at colleges and universities. If individual institutions are slow to change, groups of institutions are even slower. Collaboration in higher education requires both patience and determination to move institutions into new and cooperative ways of doing things.

Reconciling Different Needs. Collaboration geometrically expands the difficulty of understanding and accommodating different needs and goals. Reaching a decision on a single campus is often a complicated negotiation among many interested stakeholders. Making that same decision across campuses is considerably more difficult. As a result, developing processes that help to identify common goals and to shape possible alternatives are critical to finding compromise solutions that can be acceptable to all groups.

Building Strong Relationships. Also critical for achieving successful joint approaches is the relationship among the individuals within consortia. Unless key administrators and faculty members trust and respect their counterparts within the consortium, collaboration beyond the most superficial level is almost certain to fail. Because relationships are so fundamental to successful cooperation, consortial efforts are highly meeting intensive. Spending large amounts of time meeting and talking is a good way to build relationships but is not always a particularly efficient use of the participants' time. A real tension exists between these two goals that each consortium must find ways to reconcile. Nevertheless, some investment in relationship building is necessary if the opportunities of collaboration are to be realized.

The Definition of Core Operations. The issue here is nothing less than how each institution defines itself. Shared programs and services quickly raise the question of what makes each consortium member unique and whether sharing this service or that program compromises that sense of self-identity. This issue is particularly complex in academic cooperation. Does sharing a course with Smith change Mount Holyoke's core identity? Probably not. How about combining the Classics Department? How about the English Department? How about a shared science faculty? At some point on this kind of continuum, what distinguishes Mount Holyoke from Smith (or Amherst or Hampshire) becomes a very important issue and one which will set firm limits on how far collaboration can go.

The issue can be equally difficult in areas of administrative cooperation. It is easy to see the question arise in thinking about sharing such services as career counseling or financial aid, but it can also arise in areas of cooperation that are less obvious. For example, in the early conversations about sharing a risk manager, there was serious concern about whether it jeopardized institutional identity to share liability insurance policies. Fortunately, the Five Colleges were able to move beyond this and go on to share not only policies but coverages and retainages as well.

This last example illustrates an important characteristic of the intersection between cooperation and maintaining the institutions' core identities. As cooperation becomes more extensive, the members' sense of what is core—and therefore inviolate—and what is peripheral—and therefore available for collaboration—changes. The experience with shared risk management and the various spin-off collaborations it has created presents a good example of how successful cooperation can cause members to rethink what areas are available for future cooperation. However, although the border between the institution's core and its periphery can and will change, there will always be a set of programs and services (possibly different for each consortium member) that will not be available for cooperative ventures because they are too tightly bound up in the institution's core identity.

Collaboration versus Competition. Because higher education has historically seen less direct and less rigorous competition than most industries, there has been a general inclination toward cooperation. Ironically, at the same time that cost pressures are encouraging much more interest in consortia and other structured forms of collaboration, the competition within higher education is also increasing. The tensions between cooperation and competition are real, and successful consortia recognize this and deal with the tensions openly. Competitive pressures can intrude at various points in the collaborative process: as a spoken or unspoken reason to resist change, as a set of goals or institutional needs that are incompatible with other members of the consortium, or as a component of issues of institutional identity. However and whenever these issues arise, they complicate collaboration. It is to be expected that such issues will appear with increasing frequency as the competitive pressures on colleges and universities increase, both from within traditional higher education and from the emerging for-profit firms entering the higher education market.

What Makes for Successful Collaboration

Over its generation of cooperation, the Five Colleges have exemplified the qualities that lead to successful collaboration.

Simplicity. Given all the complexities of how colleges and universities function, finding simple approaches to collaboration greatly increases the chance of success. Students among the Five Colleges cross-register for courses without payments changing hands. Most program costs are split either equally or in a formula that recognizes rough differences in scale. An example of the latter is the "elevenths" cost-sharing formula for the common library information system: Hampshire pays one-eleventh; Amherst,

Mount Holyoke and Smith pay two-elevenths each; and the University of Massachusetts pays four-elevenths. Keeping it simple is critical.

Flexibility. The Five Colleges learned early in their history that a successful collaboration need not involve every member of the consortium. Indeed, some of the most successful joint efforts have included fewer than five participants, for example, the risk manager shared by the four private colleges and the joint employee health insurance program shared by Hampshire, Mount Holyoke, and Smith Colleges. Flexibility has been particularly important to the Five Colleges because the members include public and private, large and small institutions. A shared program among two or three institutions is both easier to achieve and provides later opportunities for additional participants. All or nothing thinking is unnecessarily rigid and will limit opportunities.

Every Participant Benefits. This may seem self-evident, but vital to a successful collaboration is the benefit to each participant. A joint effort in which some members benefit at a cost to other members cannot succeed for long. Any member of a consortium that does not perceive the benefits to outweigh the costs will drift away from collaborative efforts and probably should do so.

Appropriate Staffing. Collaboration is time and effort intensive. Having sufficient staff support to facilitate the joint work will make the difference between a consortium that actively collaborates and one that talks about collaborating. The Five College coordinator and her staff do more than organize meetings—although that is an enormous effort. More importantly, they facilitate group process for established groups, bring together individuals in areas of possible collaboration, and keep everyone thinking about how to do things together rather than separately.

A Holistic View. In any particular cooperative venture, some participants are likely to benefit more than others. Successful consortia are able to take the broad view of the overall collaboration rather than focusing on how much benefit is received in each separate cooperative effort. For example, Mount Holyoke may benefit disproportionately from student cross-registration (because to a modest extent more Mount Holyoke students register for courses elsewhere than other students register to study at Mount Holyoke) but carries more of the costs of risk management by providing office space and related support for the Five College risk manager. Neither the slight benefit received on student cross-registration nor the slight additional cost of housing a member of the Five Colleges staff becomes a separate issue to be resolved. The consortium continues to prosper because *on the whole* every member benefits significantly from its participation and each member contributes what it can to the furtherance of the collaboration.

Conclusion

Interest in consortia and other structured forms of cooperation is likely to continue growing. A number of new consortia have been formed in the last few years alone, among them the Boston Consortium and the Colleges of the Fenway, both in Massachusetts, and the Colltown group in Baltimore.

In addition, other forms of collaboration are increasing both in kind and in number. Project-specific cooperation is growing, such as the Gateway 21 project and other joint efforts to improve technology on campus created by historically black colleges and universities (Young, 1999). Other partnerships of various kinds are also on the rise. For example, Dean College in Massachusetts made the decision to remain a two-year college; however, it has invited Western New England and Nichols Colleges to develop satellite campuses on the Dean College campus to provide access to bachelor's degrees for its students while still in residence at Dean College ("Colleges Discover. . . .," 1999).

Cooperation has significant benefits for the broad range of colleges and universities in this country. For financially fragile institutions, consortia and other collaborations are a gentler way of achieving some of the benefits of consolidation than being absorbed into another institution or being forced to close. For institutions that are strong financially, cooperation provides opportunities to reduce costs in more peripheral areas and to provide additional support to core functions that can strengthen competitive position. Every college and university can benefit from cooperative efforts in some form; more and more institutions are recognizing the value of cooperative efforts and actively seeking opportunities for collaboration.

References

"Colleges Discover the Power of Partnerships." *Grant Thornton Exempts,* Winter 1999, pp. 1–3.

Young, J.R. "Black Colleges Band Together to Get a Jump on Technology." *Chronicle of Higher Education,* Mar. 26, 1999, pp. A31–32.

MARY JO MAYDEW *is chief financial officer at Mount Holyoke College, South Hadley, Massachusetts.*

10

One of the most critical components of the chief financial officer's (CFO's) portfolio is budget planning, especially in a formula environment. This chapter describes the advantages, disadvantages, and types of funding formulas used by states in the budgeting process for higher education and how the CFO can position the campus to minimize the disadvantages of formula budgeting.

Higher Education Funding Formulas

Mary P. McKeown-Moak

Chief financial officers (Cfos) are usually charged with the responsibilities of budget planning. At the majority of public colleges and universities and for a large number of private colleges and universities, the allocation of state appropriations as a component of budget planning is determined by funding formulas. On the one hand, the CFO might perceive the use of formula budgeting as adding predictability to the budget process. On the other hand, CFOs often perceive formula use in budgeting as intrusive, inequitable, and burdensome.

The use of state funding formulas or guidelines for public higher education reached the half-century mark in the 1990s. Despite the long history of use, controversy has surrounded the use of state funding formulas for higher education since their inception. CFOs have alternately praised and damned funding formulas, depending upon the impact of the formula on a given CFO's institution. Likely, the only point upon which they would agree is that there is no perfect formula. In fact, Caruthers (1989) notes that "formula budgeting, in the abstract, is neither good nor bad, but there are good formulas and bad formulas" (p. 1).

Indeed, funding formulas have changed from their original purposes of identifying an adequate and predictable resource base and distributing those resources equitably. From the perspective of a CFO, a good formula may be one that predictably provides adequate resources for the needs of the campus. Equity among institutions in the distribution of resources is not the CFO's goal, although it is the primary goal of formula funding.

Funding formulas have evolved over time into complicated methodologies for allocating public funds. Although funding formulas provide some rationale and continuity in allocating state funds for higher education, formulas are designed and utilized for many purposes, including measurement of productivity. Although the genesis of funding formulas may lie in rational public policy formulation, the outcome may not. Formulas are products of political processes, which implies that formulas result from compromise, and it is a wise CFO who can influence formula methodologies to benefit his or her campus by compromising when appropriate.

The use of funding formulas or guidelines in the resource allocation or budgeting process varies from state to state. In some states, the higher education coordinating or governing board may use formulas as a means of recommending to the legislature and governor the resources for each public university or community college campus. In other states, the legislative or executive budget offices may use formulas to make their recommendations on funding (McKeown and Layzell, 1994). Some states use formulas to determine the allocation of resources to each campus, given available funding, or to distribute funds to private colleges and universities on a per capita basis.

The CFO can be a player in formula development even when development of an optimal, or best, formula is complex because of differences in institutional missions and in the capacities of institutions to perform their missions. These differences do not negate the value of formulas but suggest that formulas can be used to provide a fiscal base to which (or from which) funding can be added (or subtracted), if justified. Formulas typically are considered to be enrollment driven, because they are based on credit hours, students, or faculty members, which makes it relatively easy to evaluate change. If additional funds are justified, then formulas can provide the basis to target supplemental funding. Because formulas may be enrollment driven, when enrollments are steady or decline, funding may decrease.

Debates over formulas arise because of declining enrollments and because of disagreements over the equitable distribution of resources to higher education. When enrollments decline or remain constant, methods are sought that will provide additional resources. Development of new programs and services to meet the varied needs of a changing clientele may require different configurations of resources in addition to different programs.

The student of the twenty-first century will likely have not only different noninstructional needs but also different preferences for instructional programs. The student in the new century may be taught by alternative instructional delivery methods, which require a shift in the paradigm on funding. The trend in this direction is developing as more and more universities offer courses through telecommunications technology. Virtual universities, where delivery of courses by telecommunications technology is shared among several public and private universities, require at least a shift in formulas or perhaps new methods of funding.

To accomplish the purpose of providing an equitable distribution of available state resources, a majority of states have used funding formulas in budget development or in resource allocation to public higher education institutions. About 40 percent of the states provide aid to private higher education through a funding formula. For the purposes of this discussion, a *formula* is defined as a mathematical representation of the amount of resources or expenditures for an institution as a whole or for a program at the institution. Programs in this context refer to those categories into which expenditures are placed: instruction, institutional support, research, operation and maintenance of plant, public service, scholarships and fellowships, academic support, and student services.

Many states provide funding for public, four-year colleges based on these functional or budget programs and provide funding for two-year public colleges or private colleges for the institution as a whole. In most states, however, total institutional needs are not determined by a formula mechanism. Additions are made to the formula amounts to recognize special needs or special missions. Similarly, given political structures and competition for funds from other state agencies, the amount determined by a formula calculation may be reduced to conform to total funds available.

Formula Development

The development of an objective, systematic method of dealing with the funding of many diverse institutions that served differing constituencies prompted many states to investigate and subsequently to begin using formulas. Prior to 1946, institutions of higher education served a limited and fairly homogeneous clientele. After World War II, enrollments jumped, and each state had a variety of liberal arts colleges, land-grant colleges, teacher-training colleges, and technical schools to meet the needs of its citizens.

As the scope and mission of the campuses increased and changed (for example, teachers colleges becoming regional universities), so did the complexity of distributing resources equitably among competing campuses. Unfortunately, state resources did not keep pace with expanding enrollments and the competition for state funds became greater. Because no two campuses are ever alike, methods were sought to allocate available funds in an objective manner, to provide sufficient justification for additional resources to satisfy state legislators, and to facilitate interinstitutional comparisons.

The desire for equity was a prime factor in the development of funding formulas, but other factors served as catalysts: the desire to determine an adequate level of funding, institutional needs to gain stability and predictability in funding levels, and increased professionalism among college and university business officers. The objective of equity in the distribution of state resources is to provide state appropriations to each of the campuses according to its needs. To achieve an equitable distribution of funds requires a distribution formula that recognizes differences in size, clients, location, and the mission of the college.

The concept of adequacy is more difficult to operationalize in the distribution of resources. What might be considered to be adequate for the basic operation of one campus would be considered inadequate for a campus offering similar programs but having a different client base.

Texas was the first state to use funding formulas for higher education. In 1996 thirty states were identified as using formulas at some point in the allocation process, down from thirty-three in 1992 (McKeown, 1996).

Formulas evolved over a long period of time and contributed to a series of compromises among CFOs, state coordinating agencies, and state budget officials. For example, CFOs seek autonomy, whereas state coordinating or governing boards and budget officials seek adequate information to enable control over resources. Formula development involves trade-offs and compromises between accountability and autonomy.

The trend in formula development in many states involves refinement of procedures, greater detail and reliability in the collection and analysis of information, and improvement in the differentiation between programs and activities. States appear to have used different methods to develop formulas. For example, Alabama adapted the formulas used by Texas to the particular circumstances of Alabama and continues to modify its formulas to reflect circumstances specific to it and to incorporate judicial interventions. CFOs may prefer adaptation rather than development of a new formula because of the time and cost required to do a good cost study. Accounting procedures are not refined enough in some states to permit the calculation of costs differentiated by academic discipline and level of student and to separate professorial time into the multiple work products generated by carrying out the university's three main missions: teaching, research, and service. However, no two formulas are identical; they reflect local practices and priorities.

Many formulas are based on simple least-squares regression analysis or the determination of an average cost for providing a particular type of service. Others are based on staffing ratios and external determinations of standard costs. The key to the process seems to be the isolation or identification of variables or factors that are directly related to actual program costs. Isolation of variables that are detailed, reliable, not susceptible to manipulation by a campus, and sufficiently differentiated to recognize differences in role and missions requires collection of enormous amounts of data. Data must be collected and analyzed in an unbiased manner that does not raise questions of preferential treatment for one campus or sector. For this reason, instead of institutional CFOs, statewide boards or other state agencies have been given responsibility for formula development.

There are several guidelines for creating a good formula:

- Formulas should be simple, and easy to understand.
- Formulas should be equitable, related to quantifiable factors, and responsive to the unique needs of colleges.

- Data should be valid, reliable, and consistent among institutions.
- Formula development should be flexible and provide incentives to encourage achievement of state goals.
- Formulas should be used for budget development, not budget control.
- The formula should be useful to institutions, boards, other state agencies, and the legislature.

Formula Advantages and Disadvantages

There are a number of advantages to formula use:

- Formulas provide an objective method to determine institutional needs equitably.
- Formulas reduce political competition and lobbying by the institutions.
- Formulas provide state officials with a reasonably simple and understandable basis for measuring expenditures and revenue needs of campuses and determining the adequacy of support.
- Formulas enable institutions to project needs on a timely basis.
- Formulas represent a reasonable compromise between public accountability and institutional autonomy.
- Formulas ease comparisons between institutions.
- Formulas permit policymakers to focus on basic policy questions.
- Formulas promote efficiency in institutional operation.

On the other hand, formulas do have shortcomings, and there have been many heated debates as to whether the advantages of formulas outweigh their down side. Some disadvantages of funding formulas include the following:

- Formulas may be used to reduce all academic programs to a common level of mediocrity by funding each one equally because quantitative measures can not assess the quality of a program.
- Formulas may reduce incentives for institutions to seek outside funding.
- Formulas may perpetuate inequities in funding that existed before their advent because they may rely on historical cost data.
- Enrollment-driven formulas may be inadequate to meet the needs of changing client bases or new program initiatives.
- Formulas cannot serve as substitutes for public policy decisions.
- Formulas are only as accurate as the data on which they are based.
- Formulas may not provide adequate differentiation among institutions.

Formulas reflect one of two computational approaches: the all-inclusive approach, in which the total entitlement or allocation for the program area is determined by one calculation, and the itemized approach, in which more than one calculation or formula is used in each budget area. There are three main computational methods for formula calculations: (1) rate per base factor unit (RPBF); (2) percentage of base factor (PBF); and (3) base factor–position ratio with salary rates (BF-PR/SR). The rate per base factor method starts with an estimate of a given base, such as credit hours or full-time equivalent students (FTES), and then multiplies that base by a specific unit rate. Unit rates generally have been determined previously by cost studies and can be differentiated by discipline, level, and type of institution. The base usually is head count students, number of positions, square footage or acreage, FTES, or credit hours.

PBF assumes that there is a specific relationship between a certain base factor such as faculty salaries and other areas such as departmental support services. The PBF method can be differentiated by applying a varying percent to levels of instruction or type of institution, but this is unusual. Reportedly, PBF was developed because of the perception that all support services are related to the primary mission of a college or university, instruction.

BF-PR/SR is based on a predetermined optimum ratio between a base factor and the number of personnel; for example, ratios such as the number of students for each faculty member and credit hours per faculty member are used. The resulting number of faculty positions determined at each salary level is then multiplied by the salary rate for that level, and the amounts summed to give a total budget requirement. BF-PR/SR also is used commonly in plant maintenance, and is the most complex of the computational methods.

Formulas may differentiate among academic disciplines (such as education, sciences, and architecture), levels of enrollment (freshman and sophomore, junior and senior, masters, and doctoral), and types of institutions (community colleges, baccalaureate institutions, and research universities).

States found it necessary to introduce factors that differentiate among institutions in funding formulas because each institution, if examined closely enough, is different and has a different mission and mix of program offerings. Differentiation is used to recognize that there are legitimate reasons for costs to vary; reasons include economies and diseconomies of scale, method of instruction, and class size. Differentiation has become more prevalent and more complex as accounting and costing methods improve and reliable cost data become available.

Trends in the Use of Funding Formulas

Formulas are becoming more complex and sophisticated, but states that have used formulas for nearly a quarter of a century are abandoning their use. In the place of formulas, productivity measures and other accountability techniques are being used to measure institutional performance and allocate resources. In addition, as state support for higher education stagnates, institutions are attempting to protect their base budgets by using an incremental approach to funding over the base formula-developed budget.

One of the major ways that the increasing complexity of formulas is shown is in the increase in the number of formulas within a budget area (for example, instruction) and the differentiation within the formulas. The added complexity appears to be a recognition of differences in roles and missions and in costs among academic programs. From a technical or public policy standpoint, the increased complexity can be perceived to be good. Formulas that more closely model reality— or that which is considered reality—are always preferable to more simplistic models. However, legislators, governors, and other state policymakers who are the ultimate consumers of formulas generally prefer a formula that is simple to understand.

Institutions appear to be protecting their base budgets by going to incremental budgeting in place of formula budgeting. Several states that had used funding formulas for at least a decade now use the incremental budgeting method. The base budget, however, was computed by formula, so several of these states consider themselves to be formula states. As state funding for higher education gets tighter, CFOs should be concerned with maintaining the funding they have with minimal restrictions on use. Formulas are, in effect, a zero-based budgeting method under which each institution justifies its request for state funds each year. Maintenance of the base can become the primary goal when enrollment declines or shifts into less expensive course offerings.

How the CFO Can Use Formula Budgeting Advantageously

Funding formulas are designed to recognize some of the different needs of colleges and universities because all colleges and universities are different. The question for the CFO is, Does the formula (or formulas) used in my state discriminate *against* my institution? How can CFOs identify the formula impacts on their institutions?

Formulas can discriminate against an institution or institutional type by the use of different funding rates for different institutional categories. For example, a separate schedule of faculty salary rates for research universities and another for state colleges and a third for community colleges is likely to provide additional resources for the research university. If the CFO represents a research university, then the CFO likely will favor this type of differentiation. On the other hand, the community college CFO will likely believe that the community college is the victim of discrimination.

Similarly, student-faculty ratios that are separate for research universities and for state colleges may appear to favor the research university. If the student-faculty ratios recognize economies of scale, then a CFO may think that his or her large state college or research university is being penalized.

From the perspective of the small college CFO, however, this type of differentiation may be favorable.

Formulas that recognize economies of scale in areas other than instruction are more likely to provide adequate resources to smaller colleges than flat-rate formulas can. For example, some states have formulas for student services that provide a base, and above that base, different rates per student are applied to institutions of various sizes. This type of formula is designed to allocate adequate resources to colleges or universities of any and every size.

Similarly, formulas that provide additional funding for research activities only to certain universities in the state will be seen by the CFOs of other institutions as unfairly penalizing their respective institutions. In any case, to determine whether formulas that differentiate by type are favorable to a particular institution, the CFO should calculate the formulas for each of the institutional types with their institutional data. It is important for the formula to be responsive to institutional differences but not to overcompensate for those differences.

The largest component of the budget is instruction, and CFOs should be vigilant in determining if the factors in the instruction formula favor or discriminate against their institution. Most instructional formulas differentiate by discipline and level of instruction. These formulas were designed to recognize the additional costs of graduate education and the costs of some disciplines, such as the laboratory sciences. If the formulas recognize the true costs of providing these services, then the CFO should view the differentiation as good. If, however, the differences are based on small class sizes in graduate classes, when actual class sizes have changed, the CFO may want to encourage a change to the formula. Because costs are differentiated by level and discipline, a wise CFO will be alert to opportunities to shift credit hours to higher levels or more expensive disciplines.

Because most funding formulas are based on regressions and average costs, large universities with many students can skew the state average cost of a particular discipline. CFOs should examine the underlying data to ensure that the calculation of state average cost does not discriminate against their university. In the same vein, use of teaching assistants lowers the average cost of offering undergraduate courses at research universities. Colleges that do not enjoy the benefits of teaching assistants should be vigilant in the calculation of average costs for those disciplines. CFOs should also be alert to unique disciplines offered by only one college or university in the state. Care must be taken to ensure that costs of other disciplines are not attributed to this unique offering, thereby lowering the average cost of other disciplines.

On the revenue side of the formula, the size of the appropriation may be dependent on tuition and fee deducts or other revenue deducts. The formula should recognize differences in the amounts of out-of-state tuition revenues to avoid penalizing the regional institution. Likewise, CFOs at institutions that do not receive large amounts from indirect cost recovery or reimbursement may wish to monitor formulas that provide revenues regardless of the level of indirect cost recovery. Indirect cost reimbursement provides funds in addition to those in the formula for the physical plant maintenance and general institutional overhead. In effect, some institutions may be receiving funds twice for the same services.

Formulas will never solve the resource allocation problems in higher education. Formulas cannot recognize the full range of objective and subjective differences among institutions and neither can they anticipate changes in the missions of institutions, such as those changes that will come about with the advent of virtual universities. Formulas, when properly designed, do provide an objective allocation mechanism that can provide more equity than independent funding of each institution with the power plays and patronage that inevitably characterize such allocation decisions. Determining the method for funding higher education will continue to be part of a political process that involves the art of compromise. Compromise will be necessary to preserve and improve quality and to accommodate the changing condition of education in the new millennium. CFOs can influence the formulas to assist their institutions.

References

Caruthers, J. K. "The Impact of Formula Budgeting on State Colleges and Universities." Paper presented at the meeting of the American Association of State Colleges and Universities, San Francisco, Nov. 1989.

McKeown, M. P. 1996. State Funding Formulas for Public Four-Year Institutions. State Higher Education Executive Officers, Denver.

McKeown, M. P., and Layzell, D. T. "State Funding Formulas for Higher Education: Trends and Issues." Journal of Education Finance, 1994, 19, 319–346.

MARY P. MCKEOWN-MOAK is senior associate at MGT of America, Inc., Austin, Texas. She was until recently senior financial officer of the Arizona University System.

11

*This chapter examines the work of the chief finan-
cial officer (CFO) in government relations, focusing
on the responsibilities of the CFO, methods of working with state legislatures, pitfalls in legislative
relations, and special problems faced by institutions
in capital cities.*

The Chief Financial Officer
and Government Relations

William F. Lasher, Gwen Grigsby, Charlotte Sullivan

The relationship between higher education and state government is
dynamic. College and university executive officers work with state legislators by employing their specialized knowledge to further the goals of both
their institutions and the state. This chapter focuses on the relationship
between the chief financial officer (CFO) and the state legislature, specifically reviewing the CFO's areas of responsibility, methods for working with
legislators and legislative staff, and pitfalls in legislative relations. The special problems faced by colleges and universities in capital cities also are discussed.

Although this chapter's focus is primarily on CFOs at public institutions, those at private institutions also should find this material useful, given
their involvement with state government. Of course, higher education governance structures differ across states. Some have consolidated governing
boards, some have regulatory or advisory coordinating agencies and others
have multiple governing boards with an additional planning agency. Some
have strong governors; others have weak governors. In an attempt to be relevant to many different state situations, the ideas presented in this chapter
are given as general principles rather than specific statements about each
state.

For example, it is vitally important that CFOs (and, indeed, all members of the higher education community) understand the appropriations
process employed in their state. Although there are state-by-state differences, Meisinger (1994) notes the following basic steps in the process. Generally, it begins before legislators convene to consider proposed legislation.

Staff members from the governor's budget office, the legislative fiscal agency, and the state coordinating agency all work to evaluate the appropriations requests submitted by state institutions and incorporate them into the proposed state budget. State coordinating agencies review budget requests in light of statewide master plans for higher education, examining the relationships between state programs and activities as well as levels of funding. Further, some states allocate resources directly to individual institutions; others allocate to a multicampus system or agency, which then distributes resources to the institutions; and still others allocate funds directly from the governor's budget office.

Regardless of how funds are dispersed, draft appropriations bills are continually adjusted based on lobbying efforts, committee actions, and updated information. Typically, higher education is one of the last appropriation items a legislature deals with and therefore is more subject to fluctuations in the availability of state funds (Meisinger, 1994). Given these procedures, higher education executive officers should also understand their individual purposes within the legislative process.

Areas of Responsibility

As a member of the executive staff of his or her institution, the CFO serves with a team of individuals who work to advance the goals of the institution. Therefore, part of the CFO's responsibility involves assisting the president or chancellor in carrying out his or her government relations duties. This means briefing the president on institutional financial matters, accompanying the president to legislative hearings and committee meetings to provide information on specific financial issues, and having appropriate financial information readily available to disseminate upon request. Because the CFO will probably have participated with the president and the other members of the executive team in developing the campus vision, strategic plans, and priorities, the CFO should be able to assist the president in presenting and justifying the campus legislative program.

When working with legislators and legislative staff, three areas emerge as primary functions for CFOs in today's environment: institutional financial matters, public higher education finance patterns, and specific information requirements or requests. Institutional financial matters can include information regarding appropriations, historical spending patterns, past and present financial management problems, and internal or external audits as they apply to a CFO's institution. Data for these topics should be retrieved easily, and explanations should be prepared describing the situation and, for problem areas, the steps that have been taken to correct them.

In the area of patterns of public higher education finance, the CFO should be aware of general trends in formula funding, performance-based funding, capital budgeting, tuition setting, student financial aid, and other finance issues that affect higher education across the country. If the CFO knows the financial trends and issues in other states, he or she will be able to place local patterns and problems in a broader context to help legislators understand the complete higher education environment.

Lastly, legislators and legislative staff will periodically make special requests for information. Fiscal notes or other financial impact statements, accountability issues, or performance measures are items that give legislators further insight into the work of an institution. Requests for assessments of the financial impact of proposed legislation frequently require quick response so as not to impede the legislative process. Therefore, such requests should receive top priority for response.

Working with Legislators and Legislative Staff

Many financial officers work closely with legislators and their staff on governmental policy and financial issues. In light of this relationship, it is important to note the similarities and differences between the state and institutions of higher education in how the world is viewed, how issues are defined, and how problems are solved.

Obviously, communication is a key element in these relationships. Both state government and the campus community have a common goal, to make higher education accessible to all people. They also want a quality product (Layzell and Lyddon, 1990). Though these points are significant, they do not completely unify the interests of both sides. There are differing notions of ownership, governance, and decision style that affect the relationship as well. For instance, colleges and universities are obligated to the institution's mission; legislators are obligated to the wider society (in other words, the citizens). The pace for processing information is also different. Higher education tends to conduct extensive research and experimentation; legislators, during legislative sessions, depend on quick pieces of information ("Communicating with Legislators," 1996). An anecdote or a single occurrence may be more useful to a legislator than a fully researched argument.

Working with the legislature also requires a basic knowledge of the legislative process. The governor, legislative committees, key legislators, and legislative staff all play significant roles in passing legislation (Layzell and Lyddon, 1990). The following questions are important in any given state: What is the relationship between the governor and the legislature? What is the constitutional strength of the governor's office relative to the legislature? Whose budget recommendations carry the most legislative weight? Does the governor's political party make up a majority of the legislature?

Once legislation has been introduced, it then goes to a committee that determines the fate of the bill. At this point, bills can be terminated, amended, passed, or sent to a subcommittee for further review. Smucker (1991) suggests several possibilities for bill behavior and appropriate administrative procedures to be followed during the various stages in the legislative process.

First, if a bill is sent to a subcommittee and is successfully passed, the full committee generally accepts it. Second, public hearings are an important time to build support for legislation. Third, by the time a committee is in markup (the period where committees begin to evaluate budget requests and earmark available funds line item by line item), most members have already decided whether to support particular measures (Smucker, 1991). However, it is important for institutional representatives (perhaps including the CFO) to be present during markup because committee members may still be undecided or need more information. Once a bill has been passed from the committee to the full chamber (normally, the house or the senate), it can be terminated, amended, or passed.

After a bill has passed both chambers, it then goes into a conference committee, assuming the two versions contain differences. Here selected members from both houses discuss the two versions of the legislation and develop compromises that will be acceptable to the two chambers. It is important to have campus representatives available during this period in case legislators have last-minute questions, or need additional information.

Throughout the legislative process, key legislators and their staff have great power over the fate of proposed legislation. Generally, senior legislators, majority party members, and committee chairs exert the greatest control (Smucker, 1991). Therefore, campus executive officers should build relationships with these individuals as well as with new legislators, who will be the players of the future.

Communicating with Legislators and Their Staff

To build relationships and work most effectively with state legislators, members of the campus community need to pay special attention to their methods of communication. For each CFO, responsible communication includes such principles as

- Learning background information about legislators, such as their priorities, constituents, educational attainment, and occupation
- Looking at the CFO's institution through the eyes of the legislator (What general impressions of institutions of higher education do legislators hold? What do they believe is the role of the institution: for example, is it teaching, research, and public service or simply teaching?)
- Working with and not against legislators to solve problems
- Recognizing that legislators are public figures and therefore may take certain actions based on their public status versus private concerns
- Not introducing new ideas at the capitol building, but working with legislators between sessions when there is time to explain concerns ("Communicating with Legislators," 1996).

Because many individuals at an institution will communicate with legislators, it is important for the CFO to work with the government relations representative(s) on his or her campus. These individuals have valuable insight and experience with the political process. Part of their work is to coordinate information exchanges between the institution and the state.

Providing Information. Legislators will ask for information regarding various aspects of the institution's finances and operations. In providing information, it is necessary to have a working knowledge of proposed legislation (Mack, 1989). The CFO should carefully examine all the issues surrounding the bill. What makes this legislation important? What are the consequences if a bill passes or fails? What overall impact will the proposed legislation have on the institution, not only financially but in other ways, too?

Above all, truthfulness is essential. Confidentiality cannot be guaranteed (Mack, 1989), and if trust is lost, there is little that can be done to regain a legislator's confidence. If there has been some sort of failure, admit the mistake and list the steps taken to correct the problem. As with fiscal notes, timing is crucial. It is better to provide information that has been generalized quickly than to wait too long for information that is fully detailed ("Communicating with Legislators," 1996). Information should be kept clear, concise, defensible, and consistent (Smucker, 1991; "Communicating with Legislators," 1996). Legislators have great demands on their time; one- or two-page summaries with bulleted facts or charts and tables are best.

CFOs are normally required at some point to communicate verbally with legislators and their staffs through formal testimony as well as informal conversation. Respect should always be shown to the representatives and their staff members. One way to do this is by using the proper form of address whether testifying before a committee or speaking with legislators informally.

When giving formal testimony, comments should be kept short and understandable. Jargon and acronyms should be avoided. One-page summaries of testimony should be provided to legislators and their staff (Smucker, 1991). However, testimony should not be delivered by reading the one page summary. Speaking extemporaneously demonstrates a working knowledge of the issue at hand, allows full attention to be given to the legislators, and appears more genuine. Inclusive language should be used; the issues being addressed typically affect many campus constituents. When a question is asked to which the answer is not known, that fact should be admitted—with a promise that the issue will be researched and the information obtained. After this statement is made, it is important to follow up and report back to the representative within a short amount of time.

Pitfalls in Legislative Relations. Developing strong relationships with legislators and their staff takes much time and energy. To keep these relationships strong, there are a number of pitfalls to avoid. First, the information provided should reflect the interests of the representatives. Knowing what bills the members of a committee have filed increases knowledge about their particular interests. After determining these interests, data should be prepared to explain current campus conditions regarding the particular issue.

Second, all parties should have access to and use the same information. Discussions should be based on the merits of the issue, not on whose information is better. Hence, it is important for CFOs to know where legislators obtain their figures and be certain that institutional information agrees. If discrepancies exist, legislators may become suspicious that they are not receiving a complete set of information or that the institution is incorrectly reporting or calculating the information or worse, that the institution is purposefully skewing the information. In any case, inconsistency of data will cost legislators precious time and raise questions about the institution's ability to track its own information.

Third, the legislator's understanding of the institution's budget and allocation process should be assessed. The CFO should find out whether legislators know where funds originate; how they are dispersed; and whether federal, state, or private spending restrictions exist. Assistance as a resource in understanding these matters of higher education finance should be offered by the CFO as appropriate.

Criticizing a bill without being able to provide an alternative proposal is a fourth pitfall. Legislators have many issues and constituents to represent. Presenting options will save them time and help to maintain good working relationships.

Finally, matters that are outside the responsibilities of the CFO should not be addressed. If a legislator asks for information that is the responsibility of another unit at the institution, he or she should be referred to the appropriate campus representative.

Special Problems Facing Institutions in Capital Cities. For all colleges and universities, geography can be a key factor in developing and maintaining relationships with state government. Those institutions located away from key political and economic areas in a state may find that it takes more work to develop and maintain strong relationships (Newman, 1987). Those institutions located near or in the state capital face unique challenges related to their proximity to the legislative process.

Publicity becomes an issue for the capital city college or university, especially when the legislature is in session. This is both an advantage and disadvantage. If the publicity is favorable, the institution benefits. If it is unfavorable or if the institution is seen as conducting itself in a manner that legislators deem inappropriate, the institution may suffer.

Being in the capital city also opens up the potential for the institution to serve as a model for other institutions in the state. Expectations may be higher because legislators can see how their legislation is implemented. In similar fashion, these institutions may face greater legislative or regulatory scrutiny than their sister institutions out in the state's hinterlands and may face greater danger of micromanagement.

Another problem can be basic access to legislators and their staff by faculty, staff, and students from the capital city institution in their roles as private citizens. Obviously, everyone has the right to communicate with elected representatives and make his or her opinions known on all issues being considered. Faculty, staff members, and students from capital city institutions have more opportunities to participate in the legislative process simply because they live closer to it. Unfortunately, it may be difficult for legislators and staff to view these individuals as private citizens and not as representatives of their institution. Affiliation is important and should be made clear at all times.

Resources can also be a factor for capital city colleges and universities. Data, personnel, and facilities are more readily available. Communication is easier and faster. This may lead to a situation where the institution serves as a voice for all higher education in the state. If a representative has a question, it is easy to call the local institution to gain a quick response. Legislators are also able to see the campus firsthand and observe how resources are maintained and utilized. Again, this can be an advantage or a disadvantage depending on the perception of the legislator.

Conclusion

In a time when state appropriations are fluctuating and the general public is demanding more accountability for the use of resources, it is imperative that institutions build relationships with representatives of state government. CFOs have the advantage of serving the institution and the state legislature as an invaluable resource in matters of higher education finance. They understand their institution's financial situation better than anyone and are in the best position to assess their institution's current financial health and the future impact of various legislative scenarios. They are also in an excellent position to explain the current financial context in which institutions of higher education find themselves. Because financial resources are necessary to implement virtually all pieces of legislation, it is imperative that CFOs be closely involved in the relationship between their institution and the state.

References

"Communicating with Legislators." State Higher Education Executive Officers, 15(1), 1996, available on-line at [http://www.sheeo.org/SHEEO/NetworkNews.htm].

Layzell, D. T., and Lyddon, J. W. Budgeting for Higher Education at the State Level: Enigma, Paradox, and Ritual. ASHE-ERIC Higher Education Report, no. 4. Washington: D.C.: George Washington School of Education and Human Development, 1990.

Mack, C. S. Lobbying and Government Relations: A Guide for Executives. New York: Quorum/Greenwood, 1989.

Meisinger, R. J., Jr. College and University Budgeting. (2nd ed.) National Association of College and University Business Officers, Washington, D.C., 1994.

Newman, F. Choosing Quality: Reducing Conflict Between the State and the University. Denver: Education Commission of the States, 1987.

Smucker, B. The Nonprofit Lobbying Guide: Advocating Your Cause—and Getting Results. San Francisco: Jossey-Bass, 1991.

WILLIAM F. LASHER is vice provost at the University of Texas at Austin. He is also associate professor of educational administration and serves as director of the graduate program in higher education administration.

GWEN GRIGSBY is associate vice president for external relations at the University of Texas at Austin. She has more than sixteen years of experience in higher education governmental relations.

CHARLOTTE SULLIVAN is a doctoral student in higher education administration at the University of Texas at Austin. She has taught speech communication and serves as a communication consultant.

12

Selecting peer institutions for financial and bud-getary analyses is the focus of this chapter. The key factors used to determine the extent of a peer match will be defined and discussed.

Using Peer Institutions in Financial and Budgetary Analyses

Thomas Anderes

This chapter focuses on the practical application of peer institutions as one component in financial and budgetary decision-making processes. Higher education is expected to be more accountable for the manner in which it processes information through its complex decision-making alternatives. Accountability has multiple definitions as defined broadly by legislative bodies, governors' offices, faculty committees, federal mandates, students and other constituencies. The use of peer institutions to establish points of reference is an inevitable outcome of pressures for increased input and accountability.

What Is a Peer Institution?

Webster's third edition defines a *peer* as "a person, or thing of the same rank, value, quality, ability etc.; equal. . . ." It is obvious to anyone who has attempted to define peer institutions there are few that would qualify on the basis of being equal. The differences among institutions, even those that have a number of common characteristics, can be significant enough to render comparisons of limited value.

Peer identification must always be prefaced with the condition that there is no perfect match of one institution to another. Peer analyses are most helpful when used with other decision-making processes. The most productive decision-making outcomes will generally be derived from multidimensional approaches that include peer information as one resource.

Why Are Peer Institutions Used?

Chief financial officers (CFOs) are always seeking ways to expand and improve their analytical capabilities. The demands for internal and external accountability require a sophisticated combination of tools to address all possible alternatives. How often have there been requests to link faculty salary levels to some meaningful comparative group demands to ensure that administrative programming be streamlined to be as cost effective as possible, benchmarks to substantiate that investment performance is reasonable, or studies to clarify that the amount of expenditures on students is comparable to our competitors?

In recent years one of the most significant efforts nationally in creating a peerlike comparison has been through the NACUBO Benchmarking project, which is a complex analysis of administrative activity and process culminating in a gap analysis. The gap is based on an institution's performance in comparison to best practices or benchmarks of other institutions (Kempner and Shafer, 1993).

The American Association of University Professors annually completes a survey of faculty salaries by state, institution, and rank within each institution. The data are used as a comparative tool by many states, regional organizations, and individual institutions to track progress in salary growth during the previous year.

A number of states use cost data for each of their institutions as a general comparison against similar institutions. The Carnegie Foundation classification provides a means to categorize institutions into defined peer groups; it places each institution in a broad category based on the number and level of academic programs; number and level of degrees awarded; amount of funded sponsored research; and American College Test (ACT) and Scholastic Aptitude Test (SAT), and class-ranking selectivity indicators. ("Pay and Benefits. . .," 1998).

Development of statewide funding formulas are frequently based on bundling similar institutions (community colleges, state colleges, and universities) into categories that treat the group of institutions in an equitable manner.

There are many good reasons from both an internal and external perspective to create meaningful peer comparisons. Inevitably such comparisons will feed into a planning and budget process as factors for decision making.

How Are Peer Institutions Chosen?

The selection of one or more peers should involve the analysis of multiple factors that best define the institution that it is to match. If a comparison is intended to be a comprehensive match, specifically one connected closely to a select group of two or three institutions, then there must be many factors supporting the match. (If a comparison is being made for limited purposes such as a faculty salary survey, then the number and depth of the variables can be reduced.)

In those instances where institutions seek closely matched comparisons that will address a number of purposes, the following factors should be included:

• Institutional mission
• Publicly or privately held organization
• Four-year, two-year, or graduate programs
• Number of students served
• Urban, rural, or multiple sites
• Number and concentration of degrees awarded
• E and G Expenditures/cost per student by function
• Selectivity of students

Institutional Mission. Institutional mission may be the single most significant factor in determining a peer match. Mission statements generally provide the programs and objectives defining institutional type such as public land-grant university, urban comprehensive university, rural community college, private research university or employ other mission-based nomenclature that acts as demarcation for an initial filtering. Land-grant universities will not be meaningful matches with private research universities. There may be a number of comparable academic disciplines, that is, there may indeed be peers in history, economics, or mathematics, but the connection of overall mission, source of funds, and other factors will vary such that comparisons will not be productive.

As an example, the University of Wisconsin is a premier public land-grant university with many nationally ranked disciplines. Yale University is a premier private research university nationally and internationally recognized in numerous programs. A primary objective of any public land-grant institution such as the University of Wisconsin must be to serve the undergraduate and graduate needs of the state's residents. The university clearly serves nonresidents and supports federal research grants and contracts extending beyond state boundaries. The level of state funding support for faculty and staff and public investment in facilities and continuing maintenance create an absolute commitment to supporting an array of state initiatives.

Yale University is a private corporation that is bound to the state of Connecticut only where it chooses (with limited exception in a state-supported financial aid program and academic program approval). There is partnering between the university and the state but in a manner that is similar to any other contractual partner. The extent to which Yale University works with the state of Connecticut is not due to expectations driven by financial appropriation or resident access.

Publicly or Privately Held Organization. Differences between public and private institutions are both programmatic and cost based. Private institutions rely more heavily on student tuition and endowment resources to operate programs. They expend more for financial aid than public institutions. Public institutions receive some state support for financial aid, but owing to lower tuition and fees they require less funding to support financial aid programs. As a consequence, public institutions are able to devote a higher proportion of resources to other academic and administrative programs. The nature of expenditures supporting statewide activities, such as public radio, cooperative extension, and agricultural outreach, and state-related economic development and research projects further differentiate public and private program funding.

The NACUBO Benchmarking project categorized institutions into peer groupings: public research, private research, public comprehensive, private comprehensive, liberal arts, and community colleges. The categories reflect the necessity to differentiate using peer groups as a means to better measure differences in multiple areas of cost (Kempner and Shafer, 1993).

Four Year, Two Year, and Graduate Programs. It is generally accepted that two- and four-year institutions would not be appropriate matches under most circumstances. The differences in mission, related programming, and cost mix preclude meaningful comparisons. Four-year institutions without graduate programs placed alongside four-year institutions with multiple graduate programs will have difficulty in program and cost match. The cost of providing a mix of graduate programs will generally be higher and create some distance between those institutions having limited or no graduate programs.

Single or Multiple Campuses or Sites. The number of sites or campuses comprising an institution can have a bearing on the delivery of services and attendant costs. If one institution has 20,000 students at one location, while a second institution serves 20,000 students through two full-service campuses and one storefront site, the costs of the multicampus institution will be higher. (Assuming the multicampus institution has duplicated student services and such auxiliary services as bookstore and food outlets, then its cost will tend to be higher.)

Number of Students Served. The number of students served and number of sites where instruction is provided create opportunities for economies of scale or cost efficiency that should be considered in building a peer list. A large number of students concentrated at a single site will afford an opportunity for one set of student services, maximizing space utilization and generally focusing resources in a more effective manner. Relatively fewer students dispersed between multiple sites will limit opportunities for enhancing space and service utilization.

Selectivity of Students. The type of student population admitted as freshmen or transfers is another factor that differentiates institutions. The freshman admissions filter, if set at 900 for SAT scores, will generate a very different student population than one with a threshold set at 1300. Similarly if the first 50 percent of the graduating class are considered for admission at one institution versus the top 10 percent at another, the student profile will differ between the two institutions. The selectivity factor is particularly apparent in public institutions that are frequently mandated to be as accessible to residents as possible. On the other hand, a number of private liberal arts colleges and universities establish high entry thresholds to attract only the most qualified and capable students.

Urban, Rural, or Mixed Sites. Access to services can be enhanced or limited based on the location of a campus. Urban institutions have more opportunities to create local partnerships both academically and administratively. The partnerships offer added alternatives in the development and delivery of services. Cooperative efforts in purchasing, storage, inventory control, sharing of space, and other business operations are increased when there are similar organizations locally. Rural colleges and universities must be more self-sufficient.

Number and Concentration of Degrees Awarded. The number of degrees awarded and fields in which degrees are awarded are a good proxy for institutional mission. A useful peer match would reflect some proportionality in the number of degrees awarded and areas of concentration.

Education and General Expenditures and Cost per Student by Function. The relative amount of E and G expenditures is not a particularly useful factor by itself. Analyses, which include a cost per student by function (for example, instruction, research, public service, and so on), can provide a good comparative measure. If there is a difference of as much as 20 percent in cost per student in instruction, then there is a high probability that the difference is connected to a richer mix of faculty salaries and institutional operating support. The question in the selection process that must be answered is, What is a reasonable level of variance from another institution's costs before it is eliminated as an acceptable peer?

Cost is one factor among many in the peer selection process. It may be that there is sufficient linkage in other factors to discount a difference in cost per student.

Pitfalls in Peer Selection and Use

There are two pitfalls in the selection and use of peers. The first pitfall is identifying peers that do not adequately match the desired profile. There may be matches in individual factors but differences that would outweigh any matches. As an example, the number of students served, degrees awarded, and a single campus may be very comparable between two institutions, but the combination of other factors such as the types of degrees awarded, an urban location as opposed to rural, and significant cost-per-student differential would create enough of a difference to limit use as a reliable peer.

The second pitfall is the identification of a peer so closely matched that it is perceived as a singular benchmark for decision making. It is essential that the use of peers be one of a number of tools contributing to financial decisions. Other sources of input, including formulas, cost-benefit reviews, and incremental analyses, should be used in conjunction with peer analyses.

Issues Connected with the Use of Peers

When a selection of peer institutions is undertaken, there should be clarification as to whether or not the peer list will include only institutions that match the present profile or whether identifying peers that are aspirational is an objective. Aspirational peers will be recognized as possessing various qualities or strengths not presently part of the institutional profile. The overriding goal is to benchmark to objectives of size, location, or cost that are not represented by the existing set of factors. Generally it would be useful to identify two sets of peers, one set that is closely matched and another that is aspirational. There is some advantage in decision-making processes to have a clear set of standards or objectives that you seek to achieve beyond the more immediate maintenance or short-term goals.

It should be realized that the identification of institutional peers for broadly conceived comparisons does not preclude the use of a different set of peers for other purposes. A number of peer rating processes in academic programming offer discrete comparisons or rankings by discipline. The rating process is based on many factors focusing on aspects of teaching, research, publishing, and national perception. There is a national ranking of libraries based on a number of variables that can be used in a peer review process as well.

The intent of each peer review may result in differing lists of institutions depending on whether the peer review is for an overall institutional comparison, for faculty salary equity, number of library acquisitions, cost per student comparison, and so forth.

Future Use of Institutional Peers in Financial and Budgetary Analyses

The future is bright for the expansion of institutional peers as a tool in financial and budgetary decision making. Continuing demands for internal and external accountability will necessitate requirements for comparisons to the market and the nearest competitors. State officials will be interested in the report card approach of how well institutions are faring against various benchmarks. Campus leaders will be interested in building added sources of justification as they make their cases for new resources. The use of peer institutions in supporting financial and budgetary decisions will be an important tool.

The CFO must be sensitive to the nuances of peer selection and use. The outcomes of peer application will likely maximize individual and collective abilities of institutional leadership to make more thorough and informed decisions.

References

Kempner, D., and Shafer, B. S. "The Pilot Years: The Growth of the NACUBO Benchmarking Project." *NACUBO Business Officer,* December 1993, pp. 22–31.

"Pay and Benefits of Leaders at 475 Private and Universities: A Survey." *Chronicle of Higher Education,* Oct. 23, 1998, p. A39.

THOMAS ANDERES is vice chancellor for finance and administration for the University and Community College System of Nevada.

INDEX

insurance, 87–88; replacement cost, 88
Internet access, 40, 46
Intranet, 22
Investment committees, 52, 54; optimal time use of, 57; policy decisions, 57
Investment managers, 57; complementary structure of, 58; core-satellite approach, 58; cost of, 58
Investment policy decisions, 51
Investment portfolio, 51
Itemized formula approach, 103

Jenkins, R., 39, 47, 50

Kaiser, H., 74, 81
Katz, R. N., 41, 50
Kempner, D., 118, 120, 123
Klein, E., 74, 81
KPMG, LLP, 65

Land acquisitions, 77
Land-grant universities, 119
Lapovsky, L., 15
Layzell, D. T., 100, 111, 115
Leach, K., 41, 50
Leasing programs, 42, 45
Least-squares regression analysis, 102
Legal liability, 84–85, 88
Legal services, 92
Legislative relations: areas of responsibility, 110–111; capital cities institutions, 114–115; CFO and, 109–110; communication process and, 111; pitfalls in, 113–114; working with legislative staff, 111–112
Life cycle budgeting strategies, 45
Long-range projections, 30
Long-term debt financing, 77

Mack, C. S., 113, 115
McKeown, M. P., 100, 102
Mainframes, 43
Maintenance programs, 31
Maintenance staff, 85
Management training, 92
Market timing, 54
Massachusetts Higher Education Consortium, 92
Master planning. See Campus master planning
Matching principle, 61

Measurement system: financial measures, 64; financial and non-financial performance, 63–65; performance ratios, 65; success factors, 65; suggestions for, 64–65
"Measuring Past Performance to Chart Future Directions," 65
Meisinger, R. J., 28, 113, 115
Mellon Foundation, 92
Merit-based student aid, 9
Mid-term cost containment solutions, 31–33
Mission-driven budget model, 64
Monitizing activities, 67
Mount Holyoke College, 91, 97
Multi-year budgets, 18
Myers, D., 15

National Association of College and University Business Officers (NACUBO): benchmarking project, 118, 120; endowment study, 54; Institutional Financial Aid Survey, 5–8, 14
Need-based student aid, 9
Need-blind admissions policy, 17, 34
Negligence, 84
Net income ratio, 65
Net tuition revenues, 5, 19, 29; class characteristics and, 12–13; defined, 6; enrollment changes and, 7–8; tuition and, 6–7, 15
Newman, F., 114, 115
Nichols College, 98
"90-90" rule, 47
Nitterhouse, D., 28
Nontraditional investments, 56–57
Norris, D. M., 41, 44, 49, 50
Northeastern University, 36
Notebook computers, 48

Objective budget, 18
Occupational Health and Safety Act (OSHA), 76
Off campus accidents, 87
On-line course catalog, 92
One-time funding allocations, 40
Operating budget, 19, 23; capital budgeting and, 77–78; as management tool, 61
Operating expense, 45, 80
Optimal class, 5
Optimizer, asset allocation and, 55–56
Organizational structure, 29

Back Issue/Subscription Order Form

Copy or detach and send to:
Jossey-Bass Inc., Publishers, 350 Sansome Street, San Francisco CA 94104-1342
Call or fax toll free!
Phone 888-378-2537 6AM-5PM PST; Fax 800-605-2665

Back issues: Please send me the following issues at $23 each.
(Important: please include series initials and issue number, such as HE90.)

1. HE _____

_____

_____

$ _____ Total for single issues

$ _____ Shipping charges (for single issues *only;* subscriptions are exempt
from shipping charges): Up to $30, add $5^{50} • $30^{01}–$50, add $6^{50}
$50^{01}–$75, add $7^{50} • $75^{01}–$100, add $9 • $100^{01}–$150, add $10
Over $150, call for shipping charge.

Subscriptions   Please ❑ start   ❑ renew my subscription to *New Directions
for Higher Education* for the year 19___ at the following rate:

❑ Individual $58   ❑ Institutional $104
NOTE: Subscriptions are quarterly, and are for the calendar year only.
Subscriptions begin with the spring issue of the year indicated above.
For shipping outside the U.S., please add $25.

$ _____ Total single issues and subscriptions (CA, IN, NJ, NY, and DC
residents, add sales tax for single issues. NY and DC residents must
include shipping charges when calculating sales tax. NY and Canadian
residents only, add sales tax for subscriptions.)

❑ Payment enclosed (U.S. check or money order only)
❑ VISA, MC, AmEx, Discover Card #_____ Exp. date_____

Signature _____ Day phone _____
❑ Bill me (U.S. institutional orders only. Purchase order required.)
Purchase order #_____

Name _____

Address _____

_____

_____

Phone_____ E-mail _____

For more information about Jossey-Bass Publishers, visit our Web site at:
www.josseybass.com   **PRIORITY CODE = ND1**

OTHER TITLES AVAILABLE IN THE
NEW DIRECTIONS FOR HIGHER EDUCATION SERIES
Martin Kramer, Editor-in-Chief